Food Gifts

FOR ALL SEASONS

FOOD GIFTS
FOR ALL SEASONS

Written by Anne Byrn

Illustrated by Anne Hathaway

PEACHTREE

ATLANTA

For John.
—*A.B.*

For Mr. Lee.
— *A.H.*

Published by
PEACHTREE PUBLISHERS, LTD.
494 Armour Circle NE
Atlanta, Georgia 30324

Text © 1996 by Anne Byrn
Illustrations © 1996 by Anne Hathaway

Jacket illustration by Anne Hathaway

Book design by Nicola Simmonds Carter

Manufactured in Hong Kong

10 9 8 7 6 5 4 3 2 1
First Edition

Library of Congress Cataloging-in-Publication Data

Byrn, Anne.
    Food gifts for all seasons / by Anne Byrn ; illustrated by Anne Hathaway. — 1st ed.
        p.   cm.
    Includes index.
    ISBN 1-56145-124-X   (hardcover)
    1. Cookery.   2. Gifts.   I. Title.
TX652.B759   1996
641.5—dc20
                                                    96-12492
                                                    CIP

CONTENTS

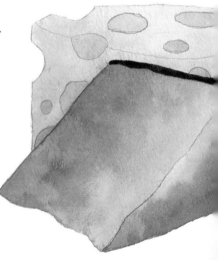

INTRODUCTION
'Tis Better to Give...

"The supreme gift is the giving of oneself... Happy are those nations where the custom of gifts has remained a vital thing."
—Dr. Paul Tournier, THE MEANING OF GIFTS

As I write this introduction for a book of recipes I have been collecting for the past ten years, I realize how food can etch permanent memories into our psyche. When we present someone with a gift of food, we practice one of life's great rituals—much like singing happy birthday, giving thanks before dinner, or carving pumpkins for Halloween. These gifts become a means of preserving—or beginning—the ritual of presenting food to others. A loaf of bread, a batch of brownies, a jar of plum preserves, given from the heart and home, mean far more to someone than just a kind gesture. In fact, taking part in this ritual of creating and sharing carries a multitude of meanings.

A gift of food is a gift of yourself. My mother had always given food gifts to anyone who could benefit from a kind gesture. Still, when my father suffered a stroke several years ago, the generosity of others surprised her. Cakes, breads, spreads, vegetables—all sorts of wonderful expressions of friendship and caring arrived at my parents' home throughout my father's convalescence. This outpouring of food gifts renewed my faith in our fast-paced way of life. Busy people still take the time to express their care and concern by sharing a gift of homemade food.

A gift of food is a gift of time. Anyone can pick up a dozen rolls or a chocolate layer cake from the bakery. But no one can make peach pound cake exactly like you do. It is this element of personality, effort, and creativity that makes a homemade gift—even if it is a bit lopsided—priceless to the receiver. In these harried days when trend analysts predict the demise of home cooking, a gift of our time in the kitchen has become truly precious.

A gift of food is also a gift of nourishment. When we present someone with a pot of soup or tray of sandwiches, we literally provide sustenance. We symbolically connect by inviting the recipient to dine at our table, making them a part of our family and our community.

So here you have a year's worth of recipes—fifty-two in all, one recipe a week—for make-ahead food gifts. I've organized the gift recipes by season so that you can make the best use of fresh and reasonably priced ingredients, and I've paired them with appropriate gift-giving times on the calendar. Store the presents in your pantry, the refrigerator, or freezer as the recipe directs, and with some simple dress-up touches—presentation suggestions are included throughout—your gift is ready to be given.

As you read through these recipes, remember that you are keeping alive a ritual that connects you to your roots, your family, your friends and, ultimately, your future.

May the recipes in this book provide you and yours with as much enjoyment as they have blessed me and mine.

Anne Byrn

January 1996

SPRING

Crunchy asparagus spears, fresh strawberries by the quart basketful, and chives flourishing in the herb garden—now those are visible signs of spring, as obvious (and as welcome!) as daffodils, azaleas, and dogwoods displaying their rainbow of colors.
As if to wake us up from soporific winter stews, these tastes of spring shout with color, flavor, and imagination.

What to do with the springtime abundance of herbs? Make a terrific Tarragon Mustard to smear on roasted chicken, or experiment with a variety of herb vinegars you can sell at the school springtime fundraiser.
For a May bridal shower, try the Fresh Carrot and Ginger Soup and Mother's Pan Brownies—the bride-to-be will clamor for the recipes. And don't forget to welcome the new family in the neighborhood with Clay's Chicken Enchiladas.

SPRING'S
DECORATIVE INSPIRATIONS

VIOLETS
ARTICHOKES
CARROTS
TULIPS
VIDALIA ONIONS
HYDRANGEA
TARRAGON
FORSYTHIA
NEW RED POTATOES
PEONIES
CHIVES
PUSSYWILLOW
STRAWBERRIES
PANSIES
ASPARAGUS
DAFFODILS
GREEN ONIONS
HYACINTHS

In the spring, the cooler-weather herbs—such as rosemary and Italian parsley—have weathered the winter and offer us a sudden growth spurt. The chives are up, and those warm-weather herbs we long for—basil and lemon verbena, for example—are beginning their stay outdoors. It's a busy time in the herb garden, and a perfect time to stash away those herbal, floral flavors in vinegars to use in the months ahead.

Makes about 3 cups

•

**Preparation time:
10 minutes**

•

**Steeping time:
2 to 3 weeks**

•

♥ **Low-fat selection**

SPRINGTIME HERB VINEGAR

6 sprigs fresh chives,
tarragon, or rosemary

•

3 cups white wine
vinegar

•

3 lemon zest strips,
about 2 inches long
and 1 inch wide,
optional

Rinse herb sprigs and pat dry. Set aside.

Place vinegar in a small saucepan over medium-high heat. Heat almost to a boil.

Meanwhile, fill three clean storage bottles (each about 8 ounces) with hot water. Pour out water and place 2 sprigs of herbs in each bottle. Add a strip of lemon zest to each bottle, if desired. Pour in hot vinegar. Cover bottles tightly and let stand in a cool, dark place at room temperature for about 2–3 weeks, or until flavors meld.

To prepare for giving, decant vinegar into clean gift bottles and replace the herb sprigs with fresh ones. You may or may not remove the lemon zest—it's up to you.

TO STORE: These decanted vinegars keep for 6–9 months in a cool, dark place. For this extended storage, you may want to remove the lemon zest so flavor doesn't overpower the taste of the herb.

PACKAGING TIP: Most giftware and cookware shops have pretty bottles for storing vinegar. Look for the handblown bottles of green and clear glass. Most of these shops also carry the corks to fit the bottles. In a pinch, recycle wine bottles and corks. Just make sure they're well scrubbed beforehand, and attach an attractive label to the front of the bottle.

Makes 4 half-pint jars

•

Preparation time:
25 minutes

•

Cooking time:
5 minutes

Equipment needed:
Sterilized jars

•

♥ Low-fat selection

Sweet Vidalia onions, in season in the springtime, are combined with red and green peppers and the juice and peel of an orange to produce this sweet yet tangy, syrupy marmalade. Adjust the heat by adding as much dried hot pepper or Vietnamese chili paste (found at Asian markets) as you like. This is a terrific glaze for pork loin.

VIDALIA ONION MARMALADE

Sterilize jars and lids. Set aside.

Place chopped onion and peppers, orange zest, and chili pepper in a 3-quart or larger saucepan. Stir. Pour in orange juice and vinegar. Stir in powdered fruit pectin. Place pan over medium-high heat and bring to a boil. When boil is rolling (which means it doesn't stop even when you stir), add sugar and stir. When mixture comes back to a boil, begin timing. Cook and stir constantly at a boil for 1 minute, then remove pan from heat.

Carefully ladle hot marmalade mixture into sterilized jars. Wipe rims and secure lids. Let cool on the counter before storing.

TO STORE: Refrigerate unopened jars for up to 3–4 months.

PACKAGING TIP: Pack in attractive glass jars, and all you need is a red or green organdy ribbon to make this an elegant gift. Advise the recipient to use the marmalade as a glaze for grilling pork or as a dip for cheese crackers, or they might spread it on morning toast! If you're feeling extra generous, surround the jar with jumbo sweet Vidalias in a pretty basket.

2 cups finely chopped Vidalia or other sweet onion (about 1 very large)

•

1 cup finely chopped green bell pepper

1 cup finely chopped red bell pepper

•

1 tablespoon minced orange zest

•

1 dried hot pepper, crumbled, or 1 teaspoon Vietnamese chili paste

•

$^1/_2$ cup freshly squeezed orange juice

•

$^1/_2$ cup white vinegar

•

One 1.75-ounce package powdered fruit pectin

•

2 cups sugar

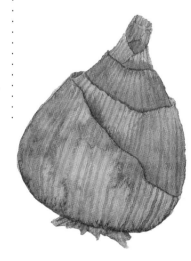

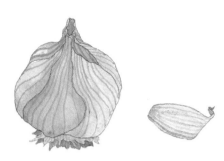

Makes 1 cup

•

Preparation time:
20 minutes

•

♥ Low-fat selection

This versatile, fresh herb-enhanced mustard is a most useful condiment—it will perk up most anything, from a bland chicken salad to an ordinary tomato. Spread it on chicken before it is roasted, dab onto salmon fillets while they are grilling, or combine with a little mayonnaise for a nice sandwich spread.

TARRAGON MUSTARD

$^1/_4$ cup whole yellow mustard seeds, finely ground

•

$^1/_4$ cup mustard powder

•

$^1/_4$ cup white wine vinegar

•

$^1/_2$ cup water

•

1 tablespoon light brown sugar

•

3 tablespoons minced fresh tarragon (or $1^1/_2$ tablespoons dried)

•

1 clove garlic, minced

•

1 teaspoon salt, or to taste

Whisk together ground mustard seeds, mustard powder, vinegar, and water in a medium bowl. Add sugar, fresh tarragon, garlic, and salt, stirring until mixture forms a smooth paste. Turn mustard into a clean jar or crock, cover it well, and refrigerate to let flavors bloom.

TO STORE: Mustard will keep in a tightly covered crock in the refrigerator for 2–3 months. For best flavor, store several weeks before using.

PACKAGING TIP: Tuck a crock or jar of this mustard into an attractive bag. On a recipe card print your favorite roasted chicken recipe or your method for grilling salmon and suggest serving the chicken and salmon with this terrific mustard. Punch a hole through the top left corner of the card and thread it with green ribbon to the handles of the bag. For a more formal gift, place this mustard in a gift basket surrounded by springtime's floral harvest—daffodils, hyacinths, pansies, and tulips.

Spread this wonderful make-ahead appetizer onto toasted rounds of French bread or slices of dense rye. Serve with razor-thin cucumbers or those wonderful tiny French sour pickles called cornichons. Vary the recipe by using other smoked fish—salmon, mackerel, or mullet—and by adding your own twist to the seasonings. I generally don't like the flavor of reduced-fat mayonnaise, but when you add lemon juice, onions, chives, and capers, no one will notice the difference.

**Makes about
2 ½ cups**
•
**Preparation time:
10 minutes**

SMOKED TROUT PÂTÉ

Place cleaned trout fillets in the container of a food processor fitted with steel blade and pulse a few times, until well chopped. (You can also do this by hand with a sharp knife). Transfer trout to a mixing bowl. Fold in onions and chives and stir. Add mayonnaise and stir to combine. Add lemon juice, capers, and salt and pepper to taste. Stir well, cover, and refrigerate.

TO STORE: This pâté will last about a week in the refrigerator. It can be frozen, in a sturdy plastic container, for about 2–3 months. Thaw overnight in the refrigerator. You will find the pâté is a little watery after freezing.

PACKAGING TIP: Pack pâté into a pretty glass bowl with a lid or cover with plastic wrap. Tape a sturdy white card to the top of bowl and label, including

serving suggestions. Tie a moss green bow around bowl and present along with a bag full of toasted bread rounds and a jar of French cornichons. If you are feeling eclectic, tie a colorful fishing fly onto the ribbon!

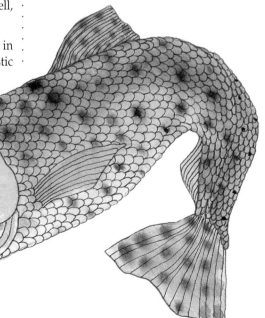

1½ pounds smoked trout, heads and skin removed and boned (you will have about 8 ounces smoked trout fillets)
•
½ cup minced Vidalia or other sweet onion
•
½ cup minced fresh chives
•
1 cup reduced-fat mayonnaise
•
1 tablespoon fresh lemon juice
•
1 tablespoon capers
•
Salt and pepper to taste

The pungent sweet-sour flavor of these pickled asparagus spears adds color and interest to warm-weather meals. You must begin with the freshest asparagus you can find, straight and tall and with compact heads. Wash the asparagus well and trim it so it will fit standing up in your jars. These spears benefit from two weeks of storage so that flavors can develop.

Makes 4 pint jars

•

Preparation time:
40 minutes

•

Equipment needed:
Sterilized jars

•

♥ Low-fat selection

PICKLED ASPARAGUS

2 pounds asparagus spears, trimmed of tough stem ends and cut to fit lengthwise in jars

•

1 teaspoon cayenne pepper

•

4 teaspoons dill seed

•

4 cloves garlic, peeled

•

2 $\frac{1}{2}$ cups water

•

2 $\frac{1}{2}$ cups white vinegar

•

$\frac{1}{4}$ cup salt

Sterilize canning jars. Wash, drain, and cut asparagus spears to fit in jars.

Pack spears, lengthwise, into hot jars, leaving $\frac{1}{2}$-inch headspace. To each pint add $\frac{1}{4}$ teaspoon cayenne pepper, 1 teaspoon dill seed, and 1 clove garlic.

Combine water, vinegar, and salt in a small saucepan over high heat. Bring to a boil.

Carefully pour boiling liquid over asparagus in jars, leaving $\frac{1}{2}$-inch headspace. Remove air bubbles with a clean knife. Wipe jar rims. Secure lids on jars.

For longer storage, process in a boiling water bath (page 80) for 10 minutes. For shorter storage, let jars cool, then refrigerate. Let asparagus stand at least 2 weeks before tasting.

TO STORE: If asparagus has been processed by the water-bath method, and jars show a good vacuum seal, the asparagus will keep in the pantry for up to a year. Once opened, it will keep in the refrigerator for 2–3 weeks. If asparagus has not been water bath processed, store it in the refrigerator for 3–4 months.

PACKAGING TIP: Top the jars with a round of burlap and secure it to the jar by wrapping kitchen twine around the lid. Attach a cream-colored label to the jar, and if you're artistic, watercolor an asparagus spear on the label.

Makes 8 half-pint jars

•

Preparation time:
55 minutes

•

Equipment needed:
Sterilized jars

•

♥ Low-fat selection

There is nothing as sublime as homemade strawberry jam. It takes peanut butter sandwiches to a higher level. It makes store-bought biscuits taste as good as grandma's. And best of all, it's a snap to prepare. Use a combination of firm and dead-ripe berries—the jam will taste terrific and pull together with the natural fruit pectin found in the under-ripe fruit.

SIMPLE STRAWBERRY JAM

Sterilize 8 pint-size canning jars and lids. Set aside.

In a 4- to 5- quart saucepot, combine crushed berries and sugar. Over medium-high heat, stirring constantly, bring mixture to a boil. Cook rapidly until thickened, about 40 minutes, stirring frequently to prevent sticking. You may need to lower the heat so mixture boils, but doesn't stick. Pour hot jam into jars, leaving $\frac{1}{4}$-inch headspace. Wipe jar rims and secure lids. Either cool and refrigerate for short-term storage, or process in a boiling water bath (see page 80) for 5 minutes for extended storage.

TO STORE: Jam will keep, unopened, in the refrigerator for 2–3 months if it has not been processed in a boiling water bath. If it has been processed, store unopened in the pantry for up to a year. Once opened, refrigerate.

PACKAGING TIP: A brilliant red jar of this jam stands well on its own. So tie a bright yellow or red satin ribbon around the jar and you're off! If you are assembling a more substantial gift, pair the jam with a dozen of Flowerree's Overnight Rolls (page 18) or a loaf of Whole Wheat Sourdough Bread (page 52).

2 quarts fresh
strawberries (8 cups),
trimmed, washed,
and crushed

•

6 cups sugar

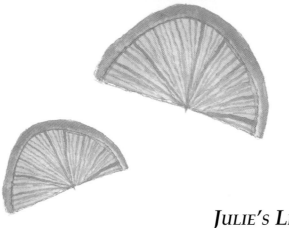

Makes 1 $\frac{1}{3}$ cups

•

Preparation time:
20 minutes

•

Cooking time:
5 to 7 minutes

JULIE'S LEMON CURD

2 lemons

•

$\frac{3}{4}$ cup sugar

•

2 eggs

•

6 tablespoons
unsalted butter,
melted and cooled

Wash lemons well with soap and water, then dry. To extract as much juice as possible from lemons, roll them against a hard surface, like a table, with the palm of your hand, or place them in the microwave oven on high power for 50 seconds.

Grate zest (bright yellow skin) from lemons and place in a mixing bowl. You should have about 1 tablespoon. Cut lemons in half and juice them. Remove seeds. You should have about 4 tablespoons juice. Place juice in mixing bowl with zest. Whisk in sugar and eggs and beat until well combined. Whisk in melted butter until well incorporated.

Pour lemon mixture into a heavy 2-quart saucepan set over medium heat. Whisk constantly until mixture gradually thickens and comes to a boil. This should take 5–7 minutes. Remove from heat once lemon curd has boiled and continue to whisk it until it cools down a bit.

Strain lemon curd with a fine mesh sieve to remove zest if desired, then pour into sterilized jars or a clean glass bowl. Cover and refrigerate.

TO STORE: Lemon curd will keep, refrigerated, for a week.

PACKAGING TIP: Pour lemon curd into any attractive glass jar with a tight-fitting lid. On label, include instructions to keep lemon curd refrigerated. Place it in a basket with shortbread, a pint of pretty, fresh strawberries, and a branch of forsythia.

This glorious, light, good-for-you soup is delicious hot or cold. Add garlic croutons and a shaving of Parmesan cheese if you're serving it hot; swirl in a dab of light sour cream and scatter with minced chives if it's cold. Tote on picnics, to out-of-town friends, or to Easter brunch for a stunning first course.

Makes 6 servings
•
Preparation time:
15 minutes
•
Cooking time:
20 minutes

Equipment needed:
Food processor

♥ **Low-fat selection**

FRESH CARROT AND GINGER SOUP

Place onions and oil in a 3-quart saucepan over medium heat. Stir and cook until onions have softened, about 2 minutes. Add carrots and stir to coat with oil and onions. Add ginger root, salt and pepper to taste, and 5 cups of chicken broth. Stir in cinnamon. Reduce heat slightly, cover pan and simmer 20 minutes, or until carrots are tender. Remove from heat and cool slightly.

Transfer contents of pan to bowl of food processor fitted with a steel blade. Process in short on-and-off pulses until soup is well pureed. Add sour cream to taste and pulse once again. If soup is too thick, add remaining chicken broth as needed.

Return soup to saucepan over low heat if you wish to serve it hot, and garnish with the croutons. Or, chill soup for an hour and serve cold with minced chives.

TO STORE: Soup will keep in the refrigerator for 3–5 days. It will also freeze for 3–4 months if placed in a sturdy plastic container with tight-fitting lid.

PACKAGING TIP: Place a jar or sturdy plastic container filled with soup into a pretty basket or decorative bag. Include a small pot of chives for garnish, a generous serving of fresh croutons, or a set of decorative soup bowls tied together with a bright orange ribbon.

3 tablespoons
minced onion
•
2 tablespoons olive oil
•
6 cups coarsely
chopped, peeled
carrots
•
2 tablespoons
chopped, peeled fresh
ginger root
•
Salt and pepper
to taste
•
5 to 6 cups
chicken broth
•
$1/4$ teaspoon
ground cinnamon
•
$1/4$ cup light
sour cream,
or more
to taste
•
Minced chives or
croutons for garnish

One of the nicest housewarming gifts you can give is a pan of homemade rolls, preferably still warm from the oven. This recipe comes from my mother-in-law, Flowerree Whitaker. The beauty of these rolls is that you can mix up the dough one evening, then do your baking the next morning. They also freeze well.

Makes about 6 dozen

•

Preparation time:
20 minutes

•

Rising time:
1 ¹/₂ hours

•

Cooking time:
10 minutes

1 cup vegetable
shortening or
margarine

•

³/₄ cup sugar

•

2 cups boiling water

•

2 packages active
dry yeast

•

¹/₄ teaspoon salt

•

2 eggs, beaten

•

6 to 6 ¹/₂ cups unsifted
all-purpose flour

•

¹/₂ cup butter, melted

FLOWERREE'S OVERNIGHT ROLLS

Place vegetable shortening or margarine and sugar in a large mixing bowl. Pour boiling water over ingredients and stir to melt shortening and dissolve sugar. Let cool slightly until warm. Stir in yeast to dissolve. Add salt and beaten eggs. Stir in enough flour for mixture to come together into a mass; it will still be slightly sticky. Cover and chill overnight.

The next morning, roll out dough onto a generously floured surface until dough is about ¹/₃-inch thick. Cut into 2-inch rounds using a floured biscuit cutter or glass rim dipped in flour. Dip rounds into melted butter, fold in half, and place in tight rows on a large lightly buttered baking sheet or on small round disposable aluminum pie pans. Brush rolls with more melted butter, if desired. Cover with a light tea towel and put in a warm place to rise until double, about 1 ¹/₂ hours.

Preheat oven to 400 degrees. Bake rolls about 10 minutes, or until lightly browned. Transfer to a rack to cool.

To store: Wrap cooled rolls in aluminum foil, then tuck foil-wrapped rolls into plastic zipper-lock bags for the freezer. Rolls will freeze well for up to 9 months.

Packaging tip: For easy giving, bake these rolls in the small disposable aluminum pans from the supermarket. Wrap them in foil and freeze. Before giving, thaw rolls, then remove foil and replace with plastic wrap. Secure with a bright yellow ribbon, and tuck into a pretty basket alongside a jar of Simple Strawberry Jam (page 15).

Clay Schaffner arrived at our house with this aromatic casserole of chicken and chilies within days of my return home from the hospital after the birth of my daughter Litton. She toted along all the right accompaniments—refried beans, guacamole, sour cream, shredded lettuce, tomatoes, salsa, and grated cheese. It was a beautiful presentation for a nourishing gift.

Makes 6 servings

•

Preparation time: 45 minutes

•

Cooking time: 25 to 30 minutes

CLAY'S CHICKEN ENCHILADAS

5 boneless, skinless chicken breast halves

•

1 onion, thinly sliced

•

1 green pepper, thinly sliced

•

2 tablespoons vegetable oil

•

2 tablespoons butter or margarine

•

$1/2$ cup finely chopped onions

•

1 cup or two 4.5-ounce cans chopped green chilies, drained

•

$1 1/2$ cups chicken broth

$1 1/4$ cups or one 10-ounce can tomatoes with green chilies

•

1 teaspoon ground cumin

•

$1 1/2$ cups low-fat sour cream

•

4 ounces Cheddar cheese, shredded (about 1 cup)

•

4 ounces Monterey Jack cheese, shredded (about 1 cup)

•

12 flour tortillas, 9-inch diameter

Rinse chicken breasts and pat dry. Place in a skillet with water to cover. Bring to a boil over medium-high heat, then reduce heat to low and simmer, covered, for about 20 minutes, or until chicken is done. Remove chicken from pan, reserve broth, and let both cool.

In same skillet, place vegetable oil over medium-high heat. Add sliced onions and green peppers, reduce heat to medium-low and sauté for about 3–4 minutes or until vegetables soften. Remove onions and peppers from skillet and set aside.

In same skillet, place butter over medium-high heat. Add chopped onions, reduce heat to medium-low and sauté for 3–4 minutes, or until softened. Add drained chilies, reserved chicken broth (adding extra homemade or canned if reserve is not enough), tomatoes, and cumin. Stir and simmer, uncovered, for 15 minutes. Remove from heat and let cool slightly. Fold sour cream into sauce.

Preheat oven to 350 degrees. Shred chicken and cheeses. Fill tortillas with chicken, sautéed onions and peppers, and cheeses. Roll up and place side-by-side in a 13 by 9-inch casserole dish. Pour cooled sauce over tortillas. Bake, uncovered, for 25–30 minutes, or until bubbling. Serve with refried beans, sliced avocado, shredded lettuce, salsa, and diced onion.

To store: This casserole will keep, unbaked, for one day in the refrigerator. If you wish to freeze it, cook, let cool, and wrap well in aluminum foil and freeze for 2–3 months. Thaw overnight in the refrigerator. To reheat, remove aluminum foil and bake about 30–45 minutes or until cooked through.

Packaging tip: Still warm from the oven, this casserole needs little adornment. Tote along little containers of salsa, shredded lettuce, avocado, onion, and refried beans for color, and place all in a pretty basket, perhaps lined with a cotton napkin decorated with chilies or other Southwestern motif.

Makes 2 to 3 dozen
•
Preparation time:
15 minutes
•
Cooking time:
30 minutes

A gift cookbook without a great brownie recipe? Impossible. Here's the best brownie method I've come across. It's rich and chewy, plus it's a snap to pull together at the last minute. Vary by using walnuts or almonds instead of pecans, or by adding a handful of chocolate chips or sun-dried cranberries in place of some of the nuts.

MOTHER'S PAN BROWNIES

1 cup butter or
margarine, softened
•
2 cups sugar
•
4 eggs
•
8 heaping
tablespoons cocoa
•
1 cup all-purpose
flour, sifted after
measuring
•
$1/_4$ teaspoon salt
•
$1/_4$ teaspoon
baking powder
•
1 teaspoon
vanilla extract
•
1 cup chopped pecans

Preheat oven to 350 degrees. Lightly mist a 13 by 9-inch pan with vegetable oil spray.

Place softened butter and sugar in bowl of electric mixer and beat on medium speed until well combined, about 2 minutes. Add eggs, one at a time. Add cocoa and blend well. Add flour, salt, and baking powder, then vanilla, and beat until just combined. Fold in nuts.

Pour batter into prepared pan and bake 28–32 minutes, or until top is crusty and brownies begin to pull away from the sides of the pan. Cool and cut into squares.

TO STORE: Brownies freeze well. Cover entire pan with aluminum foil and place in freezer, or cut into squares and freeze by the dozen. If possible, place these foil-wrapped parcels into freezer zipper-lock bags for better insulation. Brownies will keep up to 9 months in the freezer. Let thaw in the refrigerator overnight.

PACKAGING TIP: By the panful, these brownies need little decoration, especially if that pan is straight from the oven. Just include a pretty notecard and pot holder. But if you are giving a dozen brownies, wrap them in clear cellophane paper and tie up with a soft yellow ribbon. Place in a basket alongside a pot of yellow or red tulips and you have a magnificent springtime gift.

Makes one
10-inch cake, about
16 servings

•

Preparation time:
15 minutes

•

Cooking time:
1 hour, 20 minutes

MERLE IVY'S WHIPPING CREAM POUND CAKE

Preheat oven to 350 degrees. Grease and flour a 9 or 10-inch tube pan.

Place butter, vegetable shortening, sugar, and eggs in large bowl of electric mixer. Beat on medium speed for 4 minutes. Add whipping cream, flour, and lemon and vanilla extracts. Beat 2 minutes at medium speed.

Spoon batter into prepared pan. Bake 1 hour and 20 minutes, or until cake tests done. The top should just spring back when you press it lightly with your finger.

Let cake cool in pan on a rack for 15 minutes, then invert onto a serving plate.

To store: Pound cakes are good keepers, lasting at room temperature for 10 days. For longer storage, wrap well in aluminum foil and place foil-wrapped cake in a plastic bag. Store in the freezer for up to 9 months. Let thaw in the refrigerator overnight.

Packaging tip: The sky's the limit with dressing up pound cakes. Present on a pretty glass plate surrounded by plump ripe strawberries or a string of fresh violets. Enclose plate and cake in plastic wrap and then secure a bright red or purple satin ribbon around your gift.

1 cup butter, softened

•

$^1/_2$ cup vegetable shortening

•

3 cups sugar

•

6 eggs

•

1 cup whipping cream

•

3 cups sifted all-purpose flour (sift before measuring)

•

$^1/_2$ teaspoon lemon extract

•

$^1/_2$ teaspoon vanilla extract

23

In our house, you choose the flavor of the cake for your birthday party. My younger daughter Litton inherited a devotion to chocolate, but her big sister Kathleen is mad about strawberries, and so I came up with this recipe. The cake method comes from Rose Levy Beranbaum and tastes great with most any frosting—be it chocolate, strawberry, or your own family's favorite.

Makes a two-layer 9-inch cake, about 12 servings

•

Preparation time: 50 minutes

•

Cooking time: 30 minutes

STRAWBERRY BIRTHDAY CAKE

FOR THE CAKE: Preheat oven to 350 degrees. Grease and flour two 9-inch cake pans, at least $1\frac{1}{2}$ inches deep.

Place egg yolks, $\frac{1}{4}$ cup milk, and vanilla in a small mixing bowl. Whisk together and set aside.

In a large bowl of electric mixer, combine flour, sugar, baking powder, and salt. Mix on low speed 30 seconds to blend. Add butter and remaining milk. Mix on low speed until dry ingredients are moistened. Increase speed to medium and beat $1\frac{1}{2}$ minutes, or until batter is stiff. Scrape down sides of bowl. Gradually add egg mixture to batter, in three batches, beating well between additions. Scrape down sides of bowl again.

Pour batter into prepared pans and smooth surface with a spatula. Bake 25–32 minutes, or until the cake springs back when lightly pressed in the center. Let cakes cool in pans on racks for 10 minutes, then invert onto lightly greased racks to cool completely before icing.

FOR THE FROSTING: Place softened butter and 2

CAKE:

6 egg yolks

•

$\frac{1}{4}$ cup low-fat milk

•

2 teaspoons
vanilla extract

•

3 cups sifted
all-purpose flour (sift
before measuring)

•

$1\frac{1}{2}$ cups sugar

•

4 teaspoons
baking powder

•

$\frac{1}{2}$ teaspoon salt

•

$\frac{3}{4}$ cup unsalted
butter, softened,
and cut into
tablespoon-size pieces

•

$\frac{3}{4}$ cup low-fat milk

STRAWBERRY FROSTING:

$\frac{1}{4}$ cup
unsalted butter,
softened

•

4 cups sifted
confectioners' sugar,
about 1 pound

•

$1\frac{1}{2}$ cups crushed
fresh strawberries, or
a 10-ounce package
frozen unsweetened
strawberries, thawed

•

1 tablespoon
fresh lemon juice,
or to taste

•

12 fresh strawberries
reserved for garnish

cups of the sugar in a large electric mixing bowl. Combine at low speed. Add crushed strawberries and mix at medium speed until well combined. Add remaining sugar and lemon juice to taste. Frosting should be thick enough to stand up on a spoon. If too thin, add more confectioners' sugar. If too thick, add a tablespoon or two of milk.

To frost cake: Place first cake layer on serving platter. Cover top of cake with several generous tablespoons of frosting and spread to edges. Place second layer on top of first and cover with a generous amount of frosting, spreading to edge. Spread remaining frosting around sides of cake. For a decorative effect, make swirls in the frosting with a clean spreading knife, using a sharp hand motion. Garnish with fresh strawberries.

To store: If not delivered immediately, this cake should be refrigerated, where it will keep, well wrapped, for 3–5 days. If you wish to save time and freeze the cake, bake the layers and freeze them separately in aluminum foil and zipper-lock plastic bags. When ready to present the cake, let the cake layers thaw overnight in the refrigerator, make the frosting, and you're set to assemble your gift.

Packaging tip: Pack the cake in a white cake box from the corner bakery, and bedeck it with a hot pink bow and one fresh pink tulip. For a more elaborate gift, include a silver cake knife.

SUMMER

In summer, our minds turn to the beach,
to the mountains, or to the solitude of the backyard
garden. Invitations to potlucks, Fourth of July picnic
suppers, bridal and baby showers, and a plethora of
cookouts pour in.

What to tote along? Take advantage of summer's
abundance of vegetables and fruits—the recipes here
feature perfectly ripened tomatoes, fragrant basil, sage
and mint, and soft, juicy peaches, among others.

Spend some time now and capture the season's
abundance for gift-giving later—but don't forget to
give some of the fruits of your labor to you and
yours as well!

SUMMER'S
DECORATIVE INSPIRATIONS

Apricots
Chilies
Corn
Honeysuckle
Cucumbers
Mint
Nasturtiums
Peaches
Squash and squash leaves
Sunflowers
Tomatoes
Wild blackberries on the vine
Sugar snap peas
Zucchini
Green Beans
Cosmos
Marigolds
Butter beans
Zinnias

Sage is like an operatic prima donna—it likes to have the stage to itself! But talented Nashville herb gardener and cook Mary Cartwright came up with this spectacular way to spotlight, yet at the same time temper, the taste of summer's fresh sage. Even people who swear they don't care for sage love this spread! The spread needs to rest overnight in the refrigerator for flavors to meld. Store in a crock, and serve with crackers or homemade croutons.

Makes about 1 cup

•

Preparation time:
10 minutes

•

Equipment needed:
Food processor

MARY'S SAGE CHEESE

4 ounces white sharp
Cheddar cheese

•

$^1/_2$ cup fresh sage
leaves, washed
and dried

•

2 tablespoons dry
white wine

•

$1^1/_2$ tablespoons
olive oil

•

1 cup
cream cheese,
cut into 1-inch
cubes

Using a food processor fitted with shredding blade, shred Cheddar cheese and set aside. Remove shredding blade from bowl and insert steel blade. Place sage leaves, wine, and olive oil into processor bowl and process 1–2 minutes, or until sage is finely chopped. With machine running, add shredded cheese through feed tube. Then drop cream cheese down feed tube while machine is running. Blend until mixture is well combined.

Turn sage cheese into a serving bowl or crock and cover with plastic wrap. Chill overnight for best flavor, then serve.

TO STORE: Wrap bowl in foil or seal crock and store in freezer for up to 9 months, or store in the refrigerator for 1 week. To thaw frozen spread, transfer to refrigerator and let thaw for 2 days.

PACKAGING TIP: A ceramic crock or sturdy glass jar with metal-hinged top is the best storing and packaging vessel for this spread. Get creative and play up the main ingredient of this spread—fresh sage! In summertime or early fall you can break off a stem of sage and secure it to the crock with a small sunflower and some curry-hued yarn. If it's the dead of winter, decorate with some sage-green ribbon. You can also attach a little plastic bag of homemade croutons you make by slicing a slender loaf of French bread into $^1/_2$-inch thick pieces, brushing the slices with olive oil, and then baking at 350 degrees until crisp.

Makes about 1 cup

•

Preparation time:
10 minutes

•

♥ Low-fat selection

When Andrea Henry and her husband Bill moved to Nashville from Rhode Island, they eventually became farmers on their Little Marrowbone Farm near Ashland City; now they supply herbs and perennials to garden shops, gourmet markets, and local chefs. Andrea is particularly fond of basil, and to show it off she came up with this basil-lover's tapenade.

BASIL-OLIVE-TOMATO TAPENADE

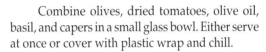

Combine olives, dried tomatoes, olive oil, basil, and capers in a small glass bowl. Either serve at once or cover with plastic wrap and chill.

Toss with hot pasta, serve atop toasted bread rounds, or spoon on top of cream cheese or soft goat cheese as an appetizer.

TO STORE: This tapenade will keep, covered, in the refrigerator for up to 10 days.

PACKAGING TIP: The 8- to 10-ounce size ceramic covered casseroles found at cookware shops are practical carriers for this aromatic spread. (After the tapenade is long gone, the casseroles store all sorts of leftovers.) Tie a straw-colored raffia ribbon around the casserole, and, if you wish, include serving suggestions—or include some soft goat cheese or a loaf of French bread for slicing into croutons.

$^1/_2$ cup pitted
and chopped Greek
kalamata olives

•

$^1/_2$ cup chopped
Oven-Dried Tomatoes
(page 31) or sun-dried
tomatoes

•

$^1/_4$ cup extra-virgin
olive oil

•

4 tablespoons
fresh basil, sliced
into ribbons

•

1 tablespoon capers

Makes 1 cup or
enough for one half-
pint (8-ounce) jar

•

Preparation time:
8 to 10 minutes

•

Equipment needed:
Food processor

•

♥ Low-fat selection

Mint is a very bossy herb in summertime gardens. Once it finds a cool, well-drained spot, the roots grow like mad and will choke out whatever herbs, flowers, or weeds are in their path. Your best defense is to harvest the crop often and make this easy mint sauce to store in sturdy glass jars and freeze. This is a delightful sauce for summer's grilled lamb chops, eggplant slices, or chicken breasts.

FRESH MINT SAUCE

2 cups fresh mint
leaves, washed and
dried, stems removed

•

$^1/_2$ cup white
wine vinegar

•

$^1/_2$ cup
granulated sugar

Combine clean mint leaves, vinegar, and sugar in container of food processor fitted with steel blade or in a blender. Process about 2 minutes, until mixture is finely chopped. Pack in sterilized glass jar.

TO STORE: Sauce will keep for a month in the refrigerator.

PACKAGING TIP: Store sauce in a glass jar. Cover the top with a square of bright green plaid cotton and secure with kitchen twine. Glue a mint leaf to a small white card, punch a hole in the card, and then secure this card to the rim of the jar.

The late Jean Thwaite was a newspaper colleague for many years, and while we came from different generations, we shared a love of good food. One of her friends, Betsy Balsley, former food editor of the Los Angeles Times, gave her this straightforward, delicious, and economical way of drying tomatoes. Home-dried tomatoes are plumper, more flavorful, and much less expensive than commercially dried tomatoes. Use in salads, soups, sauces, on top of cheese, in Basil-Olive-Tomato Tapenade (page 29), or eat straight from the jar.

Makes 2 cups

•

Preparation time:
3 to 5 hours

•

♥ Low-fat selection

OVEN-DRIED TOMATOES

Preheat oven to 300 degrees. Choose tomatoes with even red color, with no green or black spots. Wash tomatoes and remove the stem ends. Slice lengthwise into halves. Squeeze gently to remove some of the juice and seeds. Pat dry with paper towels. Sprinkle with oregano, basil, garlic, and salt to taste. Arrange tomato halves cut-side down on nonstick baking sheets or on baking racks that have been misted with vegetable oil spray. Place racks onto baking sheets.

Bake 3–5 hours, or until tomatoes are dry. Don't overdry or tomatoes will get tough. However, if tomatoes are not dried long enough they will mold in storage.

Cool tomatoes, then toss with white wine vinegar. Transfer tomatoes to a clean quart jar. Place rosemary sprigs in jar and pour in olive oil. If you are planning to use soon, store in a cool, dry place at room temperature.

To store: In the refrigerator, tomatoes will stay fresh as long as the oil does, about 4–5 months. The olive oil will appear cloudy, but it will clear up once it returns to room temperature.

PACKAGING TIP: Package tomatoes in clay jars you have sponge painted with green leaves. Or, to include them in a gift basket, pack them in a small glass jar along with a basil or nasturtium plant, a loaf of Black Pepper Cheese Bread (page 54) and Mary's Sage Cheese (page 28).

3 pounds firm ripe Italian (plum or Roma) tomatoes

•

2 tablespoons dried oregano

•

2 tablespoons dried basil

•

1 tablespoon minced garlic

•

Salt to taste

•

2 tablespoons white wine vinegar

•

2 fresh rosemary sprigs

•

$1\frac{1}{4}$ cups extra virgin olive oil

My aunt Mary Jo Ellis came up with an ingenious way to prepare peach preserves in the summer heat. Let fresh, fragrant peach slices, sugar, and a little lemon juice "cook" in the full sun until nicely thickened. You must be sure to cover the peaches with a glass lid to keep out hungry ants, bees, and all sorts of garden pests. Store in the refrigerator at night, and in two to three days you'll have the most delightful, piquant peach preserves you've ever tasted.

Makes 4 to 5 half-pint (8-ounce) jars

•

Preparation time: 2 to 3 days

•

♥ **Low-fat selection**

Sun-Cooked Peach Preserves

6 cups peeled, sliced peaches (about 6 large, ripe, but still slightly firm peaches)

•

4 cups sugar

•

3 tablespoons fresh lemon juice

Place peach slices, sugar and lemon juice into a 2-quart stainless steel or enamel saucepan. Stir to combine. Let mixture rest for 30 minutes so that juices have time to seep out of peaches and sugar seems to dissolve.

Turn heat on medium-high and bring mixture to a boil, stirring. Reduce heat to medium-low and let simmer for 8 minutes, stirring occasionally. Remove from heat.

Transfer peach mixture to a clean 2-quart glass casserole dish with glass lid or a glass bowl on top of which you can place a clean glass plate. Cover dish with lid or plate and place on a table outdoors for at least 6 hours of full sun daily. Stir once or twice each day.

At the end of each day, bring peaches inside and refrigerate. Cover with fitted lid or with a sheet of plastic wrap.

Depending on the amount of liquid in the peaches and the intensity of the sun, the preserves should come together in 2 to 3 days. The peach slices should look translucent and the juices should be thickened, although not as thickened as commercial peach preserves.

Pack into 4 or 5 sterilized half-pint jars, leaving $1/4$-inch headspace. Sterilize lids and rims and secure. Refrigerate.

To store: Preserves will keep unopened for 2–3 months in refrigerator. Opened, they will keep 2–3 weeks.

Variation: If you wish to extend the shelf life of these preserves, follow the water-bath canning method (page 80). Bring sun-thickened mixture to a boil, pack in sterilized jars, secure lids and tops, and then process in a boiling water bath for 5 minutes. Store on pantry shelf for up to 6 months.

Packaging tip: These preserves are a stunning shade of peachy-gold, so by all means pack in attractive clear jars to let their color shine through. French canning jars with a slightly cut-glass appearance look especially sophisticated. Tie some gold or khaki-hued raffia ribbon around the neck of the jar and secure a white label to the side. For an extra touch, decorate the label with a watercolor drawing of a peach.

Makes 4 half-pint
(8-ounce) jars

•

Preparation time:
15 minutes

•

Resting time:
Overnight, plus
4 hours

Cooking time:
50 minutes

•

♥ Low-fat
selection

Damson plums are the tiny, deep-bluish-purple plums you find in season from the end of summer well into autumn. What makes the Damson so delightful is its green-yellow flesh, the nip it adds to preserves, and the spiciness of the plum after it cooks down. This method is a shorter version of one devised by Edna Lewis, the skilled Southern cook and author who lives in Atlanta. The seeds are retained in the preserves for both flavor and color, but unlike Edna, I discard them before turning the preserves into jars.

DAMSON PLUM PRESERVES

Remove stems from plums and wash well. Turn plums with the water that still clings to them into a 5-quart saucepan. Pierce them with a cake tester or a long-handled fork so that each plum has two or three holes in it. Pour in sugar and stir to combine. Let mixture rest 4 hours at room temperature.

Place pan holding plums over medium heat and bring mixture to a simmer. Stir and crush plums slightly with the back of a wooden spoon to extract juice. Cook, stirring, until the plums are tender and syrup thickens. You may need to reduce heat if mixture simmers too vigorously. This will take between 30–40 minutes. Don't overcook, or the mixture will stiffen up and won't be spreadable. Turn off heat, and once the pan has cooled, place it in the refrigerator overnight.

The next morning, place the pan over medium heat. As preserves warm, try to remove as many seeds as you can. This is best done with a slotted spoon or a big serving spoon. Heat preserves until they come to a boil, then reduce heat and simmer 3–4 minutes.

Sterilize 4 half-pint canning jars with lids. Ladle hot preserves into jars, leaving $^1/_4$-inch head space. Adjust lids and seal.

TO STORE: Sealed preserves will keep up to 6 months in the refrigerator. You can extend the shelf life of the preserves by water-bath canning (see page 80) for 5 minutes.

PACKAGING TIP: An elegant way to set off the deep plummy color of these preserves is to wrap them in thin gold foil or gold mylar and secure a purple satin ribbon around the neck of the jar. If you want to present them in a gift basket, include recipes for (or even a batch of) Orange Currant Scones (page 68) or Flowerree's Overnight Rolls (page 18), both delicious vehicles for enjoying this seasonal treat.

2 pounds firm
Damson plums

•

3 cups sugar

Makes one loaf, about 8 to 10 servings

•

Preparation time: 15 minutes

•

Cooking time: 60 to 70 minutes

Equipment needed: $8^1/_2$ by $4^1/_2$ by $2^1/_2$-inch loaf pan

This is one of my favorite banana bread recipes—easy to assemble, based on vegetable oil, so it's lighter than those loaves made with butter, and it has a true banana flavor, unadulerated by cinnamon or spices. The fresh blueberries add a nice contrast, not only visually, but in your mouth— not too far from a cross between a blueberry muffin and banana bread, I think. When other berries are at hand— blackberries or raspberries—you can use them instead of blueberries.

BLUEBERRY BANANA BREAD

$1^1/_2$ cups all-purpose flour

•

$3/_4$ teaspoon baking soda

•

$1/_4$ teaspoon salt

•

1 cup sugar

•

2 eggs, lightly beaten

•

$3/_4$ cup vegetable oil

•

3 tablespoons buttermilk

•

1 cup mashed ripe bananas (about 2 large)

•

$3/_4$ cup fresh blueberries, washed and stems removed

Preheat oven to 325 degrees.

Lightly grease and flour an $8^1/_2$ by $4^1/_2$ by $2^1/_2$-inch loaf pan.

Stir together flour, baking soda, and salt in a large mixing bowl. Make a well in center and add sugar, beaten eggs, oil, and buttermilk. Stir to blend. Fold in bananas and blueberries.

Pour batter into prepared pan. Bake on the middle oven rack for 60–70 minutes, or until toothpick inserted in center comes out clean. Let cool in pan 10 minutes. Remove from pan and cool completely on a wire rack. Wrap in plastic wrap and chill for easiest slicing and best flavor.

TO STORE: This bread keeps in the refrigerator for up to 3 weeks if well wrapped. Otherwise, store in the freezer for 6–9 months.

PACKAGING TIP: Wrap a decorative tea towel around a loaf of this banana bread and it will seem to arrive straight from the oven! This recipe also freezes very well.

These delicate muffins made of cornmeal and fresh corn are similar to those brought to me in Atlanta by my dear friend Alice Baxter. I was a new mom, home from the hospital with a baby, with no idea how to manage mothering and cooking at the same time. Alice to the rescue!

**Makes about 4 dozen
1½-inch muffins**

•

**Preparation time:
20 minutes**

•

**Cooking time:
15 minutes**

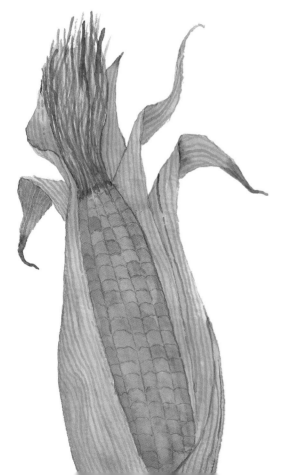

FRESH CORN MUFFINS

Preheat oven to 425 degrees.

Lightly mist muffin tin with vegetable oil spray. Set aside.

In a large mixing bowl, beat together eggs, buttermilk, and oil. In a separate bowl, combine cornmeal, flour, baking powder, sugar, salt, and soda. Fold dry ingredients into egg mixture. Stir to combine. Fold in corn.

Spoon batter into muffin tin, filling almost to the top. Place muffins in oven and bake 15 minutes, or until they are lightly browned and test done. Remove muffins immediately from pan so crust doesn't get soggy.

TO STORE: Let cool, then place in zipper-lock bags and store in the freezer for up to 9 months.

PACKAGING TIP: Pile a dozen of these muffins into a small basket lined with a cheery yellow napkin or tea towel. Include a packet of sunflower seeds for planting in the garden, and garnish with a green bow.

3 eggs

•

3 cups buttermilk

•

4 tablespoons
vegetable oil, melted
margarine, or butter

•

3 cups white or
yellow cornmeal

•

1 cup
all-purpose flour

•

2 tablespoons
baking powder

•

2 tablespoons sugar

•

2 teaspoons salt

•

1 teaspoon
baking soda

•

1 cup white or
yellow corn kernels,
fresh or frozen

When the organizers of the West End United Methodist Church's spring festival wanted to make the bake sale more useful to busy parents, we decided to sell homemade casseroles that could be frozen and popped into the microwave once home from work. Set aside a day to prepare this recipe when the zucchini is plentiful so you can put away casseroles in the freezer.

Makes 12 to
16 servings
•
Preparation time:
35 minutes

Cooking time:
1 hour in
conventional oven,
5 minutes
in microwave
•
♥ Low-fat selection

WEST END'S VEGETARIAN LASAGNA

12 lasagna noodles
•
Two 10-ounce packages frozen chopped spinach, thawed
•
2 eggs, beaten
•
One 15-ounce container (about 2 cups) low-fat or regular ricotta cheese
•
1 cup 2-percent cottage cheese
•
2 teaspoons dried basil, or 2 tablespoons minced fresh basil
•
$^1/_2$ teaspoon salt

$^1/_4$ teaspoon black pepper
•
2 cloves garlic, minced
•
2 tablespoons olive oil
•
5 cups thinly sliced zucchini
•
One 27.75-ounce jar chunky spaghetti sauce, or about $3^1/_2$ cups of your favorite homemade sauce
•
8 ounces mozzarella cheese, shredded (about 1 cup)
•
$^1/_2$ cup grated Parmesan cheese

Cook lasagna noodles in boiling salted water until done, about 7–8 minutes. Drain and rinse in cold water. Set aside.

Press excess moisture from spinach. Place spinach in a large mixing bowl along with beaten eggs, ricotta cheese, cottage cheese, basil, salt, pepper, and garlic. Mix well and chill while preparing other ingredients.

Heat olive oil in a large frying pan over medium-high heat. Add zucchini and toss and cook for about 4–5 minutes, or until zucchini is cooked through and lightly browned. Salt lightly and set aside.

In the bottom of a 9 by 13-inch glass casserole dish, spread a couple tablespoons spaghetti sauce. Place a layer of noodles on top of sauce. Cover with a third of the reserved spinach-cheese mixture and a third of the zucchini slices. Repeat with a layer of lasagna noodles, then another third of spinach-cheese, and another third of zucchini. Finally, add the last layer of noodles, then the last third of spinach-cheese and the last third of

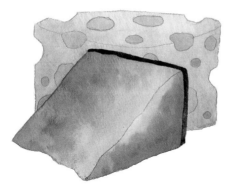

zucchini. Cover zucchini with shredded mozzarella and top with remaining spaghetti sauce. Sprinkle Parmesan cheese on top.

To SERVE AT ONCE: Bake in a preheated 350-degree oven for 1 hour, or until casserole is heated through and bubbles. Or microwave, uncovered, on high power for 5 minutes.

To STORE: Cover pan with heavy-duty foil and label. Store in the freezer for up to 9 months. To reheat, thaw casserole in microwave oven, then follow heating directions above. Or reheat frozen casseroles directly from the freezer; this will take $1^1/_2$–$1^3/_4$ hours. Frozen casseroles in plastic pans can be zapped 8 minutes in the microwave set on high, rotating pans once.

To MAKE SMALLER CASSEROLES: This recipe is great for dividing. While it makes one large casserole that will feed 12–16, it also can fit into smaller 32-ounce casseroles that feed 3–4 nicely. You will have to cut the lasagna noodles in half crosswise so they fit in the pans.

PACKAGING TIP: Gourmet take-out shops stock wonderful black microwave-safe plastic casserole pans with clear plastic fitted lids, and they usually will let you purchase a dozen or so of these pans to use for gift-giving. If not, check with the local restaurant supplier for a similar pan. In a pinch, you can use the small aluminum pans from the supermarket and cover them with foil. A bright striped or plaid ribbon makes your gift casually festive. You can also include a recipe card, but only if you wish to divulge your secret formula!

Susan Nicholson is a microwave and low-fat cooking whiz who lives in Atlanta. She passed along this easy, healthy, inexpensive recipe when I was writing a "Cheap Eats" column for the Atlanta Journal-Constitution. What I find interesting about this meatless meal is that even meat-lovers ask for seconds, and it uses up all the bounty of the summer garden. Feel free to omit or vary what you like.

Makes 8 servings
(or about 2 quarts)

•

Preparation time:
20 minutes

•

Cooking time:
40 to 45 minutes

•

♥ Low-fat selection

SUSAN'S VEGETARIAN CHILI

1 cup chopped onion
(about 1 medium)

•

2 cups finely
chopped carrots
(about 3 medium)

•

2 cloves garlic, minced

•

$^1/_2$ red bell pepper,
coarsely chopped

•

$^1/_2$ green bell pepper,
coarsely chopped

•

$^1/_2$ jalapeno pepper,
finely chopped, seeds
and veins removed

•

1 tablespoon olive oil

•

Two 15$^1/_2$-ounce cans
(about 4 cups) pinto
or kidney beans,
slightly drained

•

1 cup corn, fresh,
frozen, or canned

•

2 teaspoons
chili powder

•

2 teaspoons
ground cumin

•

$^1/_2$ teaspoon salt

•

One 28-ounce can
tomatoes, crushed and
slightly drained

•

4 tablespoons water
or red wine

•

1 zucchini, halved
lengthwise and sliced
$^1/_4$-inch thick

•

4 ounces low-fat or
regular sharp Cheddar
cheese, shredded
(about 1 cup)

•

STOVETOP VERSION: Place onion, carrots, garlic, peppers, and olive oil in a 3-quart saucepan. Heat over medium-high heat until onion almost browns, then reduce heat to medium and cook and stir for 5–6 minutes, or until vegetables soften.

Add beans, corn, chili powder, cumin, salt, tomatoes, and water or wine. (If you like your chili on the thick side, drain at least half of the liquid from the beans.) Stir to combine. Place lid on pan and simmer over medium-low heat 30 minutes. Add zucchini and cover and simmer another 3–4 minutes, so zucchini is still slightly crisp.

To serve, ladle into bowls and sprinkle servings with shredded cheese.

MICROWAVE VERSION: Combine onion, carrots, garlic, peppers, and oil in a 2- to 3-quart microwave-safe container. Cover. Cook on high 6–8 minutes, or until vegetables are soft. Stir. Add beans, corn, chili powder, cumin, salt, tomatoes, and water or wine. Mix well, cover and cook on high for 10 minutes, then reduce heat to medium and cook 5 minutes. Stir in zucchini, cover, and cook on high 2–3 minutes. Garnish with shredded cheese.

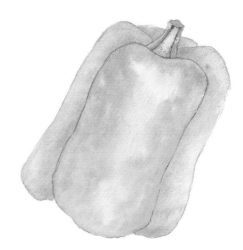

To store: Omit cheese and ladle into freezer containers. Secure lids and label. Store in freezer for up to 12 months. The sooner you use this chili, the fresher it will taste and the less moisture loss it will undergo in the freezer.

Packaging tip: Store this chili in plastic tub with secure lid, and wrap in parchment paper and a red ribbon. Send along a bag of fresh hot chilies, a wedge of sharp Cheddar, or a dozen or more Fresh Corn Muffins (page 35).

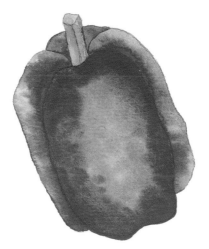

Makes 8 servings

•

Preparation time:
15 minutes if using
fresh corn, 5 if
using frozen

•

Cooking time:
10 minutes

Nashville's Nancy Bradshaw says this is "absolutely the simplest way to make fried corn," and it has become her signature dish. Nancy tired of the ordinary meat and cheese platters, so she came up with this recipe to take to meals either before or after funeral services, and named the corn accordingly. She's had long-distance calls from folks searching for that "funeral corn." While the recipe is a real time-saver when you've frozen your own summer corn or when you can get your hands on frozen Silver Queen corn, it's divine when you use fresh corn.

BEREAVEMENT CORN

4 cups fresh or frozen
white Silver Queen or
shoepeg corn kernels

•

$^{1}/_{2}$ cup unsalted butter
or margarine

•

One 5-ounce can
evaporated milk
(reduced fat is fine)

•

Water to fill milk can

•

1 heaping
tablespoon cornstarch

•

1 heaping
teaspoon sugar

•

Salt and freshly
ground pepper
to taste

If using fresh corn, cut kernels from ears, being careful to remove all of the corn's silk. If using frozen corn, remove from freezer.

Place butter in a large frying pan over medium-high heat and melt. Add fresh or frozen corn and stir to combine with butter or margarine. Add evaporated milk, water to fill empty can of milk, cornstarch, sugar, and salt and pepper to taste.

Cook, stirring constantly, until mixture begins to thicken up. This will take from 5–6 minutes, and it will get quite thick. Adjust seasoning, and serve.

TO STORE: Although this corn is best fresh from the stove, you can freeze it in a sturdy plastic container for up to 6 months.

PACKAGING TIP: If you're taking this corn to a friend's house, pile it onto your finest microwave-safe platter and wrap loosely with plastic wrap. Include a small plastic bag or other container with clean garnish—parsley, chives, or thyme sprigs. If it's the peak of summer, include a couple of ripe tomatoes to slice. Secure a note card with instructions to heat the platter of corn in the microwave for a few minutes before serving.

No dessert recipe has been the source of so much bewilderment as this peach pound cake. When it is good—made with ripe, but still-firm peaches—it is very, very good. But when it is made with those dead-ripe, drip-down-your-arm-to-your-elbow peaches, it is downright tricky. Play it safe and drain the peaches before adding to the batter. Bake in smaller pans and freeze for future gift-giving.

Makes 12 to 16 servings
•
Preparation time: 25 minutes
•
Cooking time: 65 to 75 minutes

Equipment needed: 10-inch tube pan or several small loaf pans

FAMOUS PEACH POUND CAKE

Preheat oven to 350 degrees.

Lightly grease and flour a 10-inch tube pan and set aside.

In the bowl of an electric mixer set on medium speed, cream butter and sugar until light and fluffy. Add eggs, one at a time, beating well after each addition.

In a separate smaller bowl, combine sifted flour, soda, and salt. Set aside. Combine sour cream and chopped peaches in another small bowl.

Fold dry ingredients into creamed mixture alternately with sour cream and peaches, beginning and ending with dry ingredients. Stir in vanilla, then almond extract if desired.

Pour batter into prepared pan and bake on middle oven rack for 65–75 minutes, or until cake tests done. It should just release itself from the edge of the pan, be golden brown, and spring back in the center when lightly touched. Let cake cool in pan 10 minutes, then turn out onto rack to finish cooling.

TO STORE: Cake will freeze, well wrapped in aluminum foil and then tucked into a zipper-lock bag, for 6–9 months.

PACKAGING TIP: One of the easiest wrappings for this wonderful gift is clear cellophane paper (or green during the Christmas holidays), secured with a peach satin bow and one peach or coral-colored zinnia. If you choose to divide the recipe into smaller cakes, pour the batter into fluted tins and present the cake in the decorative pan, or bake as miniature loaves.

1 cup unsalted butter, softened
•
3 cups sugar
•
6 eggs, room temperature
•
3 cups all-purpose flour, sifted after measuring
•
$^1/_4$ teaspoon baking soda
•
$^1/_4$ teaspoon salt
•
$^1/_2$ cup sour cream
•
2 cups peeled, finely chopped, well-drained fresh peaches
•
1 teaspoon vanilla extract
•
$^1/_2$ teaspoon almond extract, optional

What to present to a friend who seems to have everything? A cake. An intense, dense, fudge-like chocolate cake studded with summer's fresh apricots (or dried apricots if you must). The crackly crust makes a nice contrast to the soft interior; dress up that crust with a sprinkling of powdered sugar before serving. Slice ever so thinly because it's deliciously rich.

Makes 12 servings

•

Preparation time:
30 minutes

•

Cooking time:
50 to 60 minutes

Equipment needed:
10-inch
springform pan

CHOCOLATE APRICOT CAKE

1 cup peeled, coarsely chopped, fresh apricots or $1/2$ cup chopped, dried apricots

•

5 tablespoons bourbon

•

12 ounces semisweet chocolate, coarsely chopped

•

1 cup unsalted butter, softened

•

2 cups sugar

•

6 eggs, room temperature, separated

•

1 cup all-purpose flour

•

Powdered sugar for garnish

•

Cocoa to dust pan

Preheat oven to 350 degrees.

Lightly butter a 10-inch springform pan. Dust pan with cocoa and tap out excess.

In a small bowl, combine apricots and bourbon and set aside to soak for 15 minutes. Then drain apricot slices and reserve fruit and bourbon.

In the top of a double boiler set over hot—but not simmering—water, melt together chocolate and bourbon, stirring occasionally. Remove the bowl from the heat and cool until warm to the touch.

In the large bowl of an electric mixer set at medium-high, beat butter and sugar together until light and fluffy. Add egg yolks, one at a time, beating until you no longer see the yellow yolk. Reduce mixer speed to low and beat in flour just to combine. Set aside.

In a large grease-free bowl, beat egg whites with an electric mixer or by hand until they form stiff shiny peaks. Fold a quarter of the egg whites into the chocolate mixture to lighten it. Then fold in remaining egg whites.

Fold butter and flour mixture into the egg white mixture, then fold in the drained apricots.

Scrape batter into prepared pan and bake on the middle rack for 50–60 minutes, or until the top is crusty and cracked and the interior is still slightly moist. Remove cake to a wire rack to cool completely. Remove sides and bottom of the springform pan and transfer cake to a serving plate.

Dust with powdered sugar, and either serve or package to give.

TO STORE: This cake freezes wonderfully. Wrap well in aluminum foil and then secure in a plastic bag. Store for up to 6 months. For shorter storage, keep up to 2 weeks, tightly wrapped, in the refrigerator.

PACKAGING TIP: Purchase white cake boxes from the nearby bakery for presenting this cake to friends. Wrap apricot-hued satin ribbon in a neat bow around box, and attach a small chocolate bar as a clue to what's inside.

AUTUMN

Even if the nip wasn't in the morning air and the oak trees didn't change to their bright yellow-gold, I would know autumn had arrived by the appearance of apple stands on the side of the road, the sound of cranberries popping in a hot saucepan, and the smell of fresh pecans toasting in the oven. These visible, audible, and aromatic signs of fall not only trigger our senses into action, but they also form the foundation of fall food gifts.

Football game tailgate parties, leaf-watching day trips, bake sales, and Thanksgiving are all perfect times to try out these autumn recipes. Cut date nut bread and pimento cheese sandwiches into leaf shapes with cookie cutters to tote along on any outing, or present a jar of cranberry chutney to your Thanksgiving hostess—you're bound to find many ways to use these recipes!

AUTUMN'S
DECORATIVE INSPIRATIONS

FALL LEAVES
PINE CONES
MAGNOLIA SEED PODS
DRIED FRUITS
CRANBERRIES
WHOLE PECANS
WALNUTS
GRAPEVINE
VIRGINIA CREEPER
PINE BRANCHES
APPLES
CHESTNUTS
INDIAN CORN
PECANS
GOURDS
PUMPKINS
CHRYSANTHEMUMS

Years ago my friend Judy Landy and I decided to make gifts for all of our canine and feline friends. (Obviously, this was before I had children!) We bought most of the ingredients at a health food store, and even found bone- and cat-shaped cookie cutters to stamp out the little morsels. We conducted some test market research (our pups Chelsea and Tasha wolfed 'em down), then packaged the biscuits for giving. They were a hit!

Makes about
2 dozen biscuits
•
Preparation time:
40 minutes
•
Cooking time:
30 minutes

PET PLEASERS

1 egg
•
1 1/2 tablespoons
minced onion flakes
•
1 teaspoon light brown
sugar
•
3 tablespoons liver
powder (found at health
food stores)
•
1 cup yellow cornmeal
•
1 cup whole wheat flour
•
1/2 cup wheat germ
•
1/2 cup powdered milk
•
1/2 teaspoon salt
•
6 tablespoons margarine,
chilled bacon fat, or
vegetable shortening
•
Water as needed

In a small mixing bowl, combine egg, onion flakes, brown sugar, and liver powder. Set aside for 20 minutes for onion to soften.

Preheat oven to 325 degrees. In a larger bowl, stir together cornmeal, flour, wheat germ, powdered milk, and salt. Cut in margarine or shortening with two knives or a pastry cutter until mixture resembles coarse meal. Stir in egg mixture. Add enough water (about 1/2 cup) to make a stiff dough. Knead on a floured surface until dough is smooth and pliable.

Roll out dough to 1/2-inch thickness. Cut with bone- or mouse-shaped cookie cutters. If you can't locate appropriate cookie cutters at a cookware shop, just cut into rounds or stars.

Place on an ungreased baking sheet and bake until lightly browned, about 30 minutes.

Remove biscuits to a rack to cool completely before packaging.

TO STORE: Much like cookies, these biscuits will keep in a tightly covered container in the freezer for 9–12 months.

PACKAGING TIP: These cute little biscuits could be stashed into a new ceramic food bowl for your favorite doggie. Or they might be tucked into a basket with a squeaky playtoy for a cherished cat. Whatever you do, keep them up high, because both dogs and cats will sniff them out!

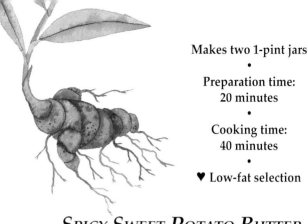

Makes two 1-pint jars

•

Preparation time:
20 minutes

•

Cooking time:
40 minutes

•

♥ Low-fat selection

The age-old method of simmering fruit with sugar and spices until it has thickened into a spreadable butter is equally delicious with vegetables such as sweet potatoes. This butter can not only act as a condiment—dolloped on grilled chicken breasts or roasted pork tenderloin—but also can be poured into pie crusts to bake and serve as a last-minute, low-fat autumn dessert.

SPICY SWEET POTATO BUTTER

Place sweet potato cubes into a 2$^1/_2$-quart saucepan with 1 cup water. Bring to a boil, then reduce heat, cover, and simmer 20–25 minutes, or until potatoes test done. Drain water.

Mash sweet potatoes well in pan while they are still hot. Stir in sugar, orange juice, grated orange rind, nutmeg, and ginger.

Place pan over medium-low heat and simmer, uncovered, stirring constantly, for 15–20 minutes. Sweet potato mixture should be quite thick but nice and smooth. Remove from heat and taste for seasoning. If desired, add a pinch more nutmeg or ginger. Stir well.

Pour into sterilized, hot canning jars, leaving a $^1/_4$-inch headspace at top of jars. Wipe jar rims and adjust lids. Let cool on counter, then refrigerate.

AS A PIE FILLING: Each 8-ounce jar makes enough for one 9-inch pie or about 8 tart shells. Fill unbaked crusts and bake at 375 degrees until crust is lightly browned and filling has warmed through. Serve warm with a dollop of lightly sweetened whipped cream or a small scoop of vanilla ice cream for a truly wonderful dessert.

TO STORE: Butter will keep up to 10 days in refrigerator or store for 3–6 months in the freezer.

PACKAGING TIP: Line a bag or basket with autumn leaves and place a jar of sweet potato butter inside. Decorate your creation with black and orange ribbons for Halloween.

2$^1/_2$ pounds fresh
sweet potatoes, peeled
and cut into 1-inch
cubes (about 4 cups
of cubes)

•

1 cup sugar

•

$^1/_2$ cup freshly
squeezed orange juice

•

1 teaspoon grated
orange rind

•

$^1/_4$ teaspoon
grated nutmeg

•

$^1/_8$ teaspoon
ground ginger

1¹/₂ cups water

•

1¹/₂ cups sugar

•

³/₄ cup finely chopped
onion

•

1 tablespoon
minced garlic

•

2 teaspoons cinnamon

•

³/₄ teaspoon
ground cloves

•

¹/₂ teaspoon salt

•

¹/₂ cup apple
cider vinegar

•

¹/₄ teaspoon
cayenne pepper

•

1¹/₂ cups (one
12-ounce bag fresh
cranberries, rinsed and
picked over)

•

1 cup white or
dark raisins

•

1 cup finely chopped
apples or dates

•

¹/₂ teaspoon
ground ginger

•

¹/₂ cup light brown sugar

Makes 5 half-pint jars

•

**Preparation time:
20 minutes**

•

**Cooking time:
20 minutes**

•

♥ **Low-fat selection**

My husband John's godmother, Mary Ferguson of Lookout Mountain, Tennessee, gave us a jar of this marvelous cranberry chutney one Christmas. The original recipe featured dates instead of apples. I find that in our house there is always an apple in the fruit bowl, but I might have to make a special trip to the supermarket for dates. Suit yourself!

MARY'S CRANBERRY CHUTNEY

Place water, sugar, onion, garlic, cinnamon, cloves, salt, vinegar, and cayenne pepper into a 2-quart saucepan. Bring to a boil over medium-high heat, stirring constantly. Reduce heat and simmer, uncovered, for 5 minutes.

Add cranberries, raisins, apples or dates, ginger, and brown sugar to mixture in saucepan. Simmer, uncovered, stirring occasionally, for 15 minutes longer.

Pour into a glass dish and let cool for 15 minutes, then store in the refrigerator for at least 2 hours to cool completely.

NOTE: If you wish to turn chutney into jars, pour while hot into sterilized canning jars. Seal with sterilized lids and rings and let cool on counter one hour.

TO STORE: Store in refrigerator for 6–9 months. To store on the pantry shelf, follow the directions for water-bath canning (page 80) for 5 minutes.

PACKAGING TIP: Pack this chutney into the most elegant canning jars you can find. Look for the Italian jars with round and exotic shapes. Secure an elegant organdy cranberry-colored ribbon around the neck of the jar. Then stick a white label to the front of the jar and personalize using a gold felt-tip marker.

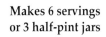

Each and every time I make applesauce, it turns out differently! This has to do with the apples, the seasonings, and the folks who eat the applesauce. Children tend to like it sweet, while adults usually like the applesauce more tart. Add a smidgen of vanilla if the apples lack flavor, use brown sugar if they need some depth, and add a little butter, if desired, for extra smoothness.

**Makes 6 servings
or 3 half-pint jars**

•

**Preparation time:
45 minutes**

•

**Cooking time:
25 minutes**

•

♥ **Low-fat selection**

OLD-FASHIONED APPLESAUCE

49

Peel, core, and quarter apples. Place in a large saucepan with sugar, water, lemon juice, cinnamon, and nutmeg. Cook over medium-high heat until boiling, then reduce heat to low and cook, uncovered, stirring frequently, until applesauce is mushy. This will take about 20 minutes, depending on the type of apples. Taste and add vanilla, if desired. Add butter if desired. Mash applesauce with the back of a large spoon or a potato masher until smooth. Continue to cook another 5 minutes.

To store: While hot, pack into sterilized canning jars, leaving $^1/_4$-inch headspace. Sterilize lids and rims and secure. Refrigerate. Applesauce will keep unopened in the refrigerator for 2 months. Opened, it will keep a week.

Packaging tip: Pile crisp eating apples and pine cones into a rustic basket, then position a jar of applesauce right in the middle.

Note: Granny Smith apples are firm, tart, and tangy, a Rome Beauty is softer and more mellow, while Jonathans and Arkansas Blacks fall somewhere between the extremes.

3 pounds tart
cooking apples

•

1 cup sugar (white or
light brown)

•

$^1/_2$ cup water

•

1 to 2 tablespoons
fresh lemon juice, or
to taste

•

$^1/_4$ teaspoon
cinnamon

•

$^1/_8$ teaspoon nutmeg

•

Few drops of vanilla
extract, if desired

•

1 tablespoon butter,
if desired

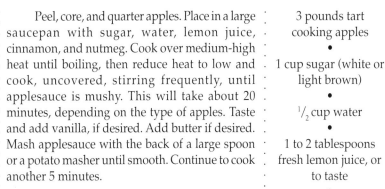

Makes 3 cups

•

Preparation time:
25 minutes

10 ounces reduced-fat sharp Cheddar cheese, shredded (about 2 $^1/_2$ cups)

•

8 ounces Monterey Jack, Velveeta, or American cheese, shredded (about 2 cups)

•

8 ounces fat-free cream cheese, cut into 1-inch cubes

•

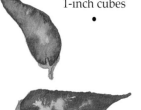

$^1/_2$ cup (one 4-ounce jar) diced pimentos, drained

•

1 to 2 tablespoons grated fresh onion

•

1 teaspoon Worcestershire sauce

•

1 teaspoon prepared horseradish

•

Few drops liquid hot pepper sauce

•

$^1/_2$ cup reduced-fat mayonnaise

HOMEMADE PIMENTO CHEESE

In a large mixing bowl, combine shredded Cheddar, shredded Monterey, Velveeta, or American, and cubes of cream cheese. With electric mixer set at medium-low, blend cheeses together until mixture comes into a mass. Stop beating and scrape cheese mixture from beaters.

Add drained pimentos, grated onion, Worcestershire sauce, horseradish, and liquid hot pepper sauce to cheese mixture. Stir to combine. Add mayonnaise and mix until a spreading consistency.

Wrap and chill.

TO STORE: Mixture will keep in refrigerator for 10 days.

PACKAGING TIP: Margaret packages this pimento cheese in small canning jars. Tie a bright red grosgrain ribbon around the neck of the jar, and this is a welcome gift, indeed! If you want to gussy it up, pack into a French canning jar with metal clamp. Place in a cloth-lined basket along with a loaf of Date Nut Bread (page 55) and a few sprigs of pine. As a finishing touch, include a pretty butter knife for spreading.

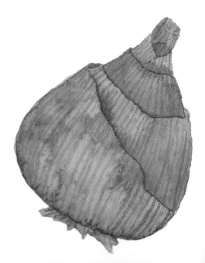

Makes 4 servings

•

Preparation time:
20 minutes

•

Cooking time:
1 hour, 35 minutes

•

♥ Low-fat selection

51

One wintry January day, I cleaned out my refrigerator and made soup—and the result was this wonderful, comforting, and penny-pinching porridge of root vegetables, beans, and smoked turkey. The recipe was a hit in my "Cheap Eats" column!

REFRIGERATOR VEGETABLE SOUP

Place turkey legs, lima beans, onion, garlic, thyme, and bay leaf in a 4-quart pot with 5 cups cold water. Bring to a boil over medium-high heat. Reduce heat to medium-low and simmer, covered, for 50 minutes. Season with salt and pepper.

Then add carrots, turnips, potatoes, and cabbage to pot. Add more water if needed. Cook another 45 minutes, covered. Remove turkey legs and take meat off the bones.

Return meat to cooking pot and stir to combine.

Serve soup with crusty bread.

TO STORE: Leftovers will keep 3–4 days in refrigerator or can be frozen in a sturdy plastic or Pyrex container for up to 9 months.

PACKAGING TIP: Give this soup in a sturdy plastic container and the soup can go straight into the microwave or the freezer. For a dressier look, tote the container of soup in a decorative gift bag with a loaf of Whole Wheat Sourdough Bread (page 52).

2 smoked turkey
legs or 12 ounces
smoked ham

•

1 cup dried
lima beans

•

1 large onion,
chopped

•

2 cloves garlic,
minced

•

Pinch dried thyme

•

1 bay leaf

Salt and pepper
to taste

•

2 carrots, peeled and
sliced crosswise

•

1 turnip, peeled
and chopped into
$1/_2$-inch cubes

•

1 large potato,
peeled and cut into
$1/_2$-inch cubes

•

1 cup green cabbage,
shredded

Makes 2 large loaves

•

Preparation time
(for starter):
3 days

•

Preparation time
(for bread):
2 hours

Cooking time:
35 minutes

•

♥ Low-fat selection

Why is it that every time I make bread I wonder why I don't do it more often? What's the fuss over some flour, yeast, and water? But the truth is that I am not alone. Many folks put off making homemade bread. Here is a wonderful recipe that just might bring regular bread-making sessions to your home.

WHOLE WHEAT SOURDOUGH BREAD

SOURDOUGH STARTER:

1 tablespoon
active dry yeast
(a 1¼-ounce package)

•

3 cups warm water
(105–115 degrees F)

•

3½ cups
all-purpose flour

BREAD:

1½ cups
boiling water

•

½ cup vegetable
shortening or
margarine

•

1 tablespoon active
dry yeast (a
1¼-ounce package)

•

1 teaspoon sugar

•

1 egg, well beaten

•

½ cup sugar

•

½ teaspoon salt

•

1 cup Sourdough
Starter (at room
temperature)

•

3 cups all-purpose
flour, divided use

•

2 cups
whole-wheat flour

FOR THE SOURDOUGH STARTER: Combine yeast and warm water. Set aside 5 minutes. Gradually add flour, beating at medium speed with ab electric mixer until smooth. Cover with plastic wrap. Place in a warm spot until bubbles appear on the surface. This will take about 24 hours. If starter doesn't begin to ferment after 24 hours, discard it and start over.

Stir starter well, cover, and return to a warm place. Let stand 2 days or until foamy. Stir well, pour into an airtight plastic or glass container, and store in refrigerator. Stir well and let come to room temperature before using. Makes 4 cups starter.

TO FEED STARTER: Starter should be used once a week. If you do not use the starter, feed it with 1 teaspoon sugar and stir well to keep the yeast alive.

53

FOR THE BREAD: Combine boiling water and shortening or margarine in a large mixing bowl. Let cool to 105–115 degrees F. Add yeast and 1 teaspoon sugar. Stir and let stand 15 minutes. Add beaten egg, $^1/_2$ cup sugar, salt, Sourdough Starter, and $2^1/_2$ cups of all-purpose flour. Beat with an electric mixer at medium speed for 3 minutes. Gradually stir in remaining $^1/_2$ cup all-purpose flour and whole wheat flour.

Turn dough out onto a floured surface and knead 5 minutes or until smooth and elastic. Place dough into a greased bowl, turning dough to oil all sides. Cover bowl with plastic wrap and place in a warm spot, such as near the back burner of a gas stove or in a bathroom. Let rise until doubled in bulk, about $1^1/_2$ to 2 hours.

Punch down dough and divide in half. Place each half of dough on a floured surface. Roll each half into an 8 by 18-inch rectangle. Roll up, beginning at narrow edge. Pinch seams and edges together to seal. Place seam-side down in two well-greased 9 by 5-inch loaf pans.

Cover pans and let dough rise in a warm place until doubled in bulk, about 1 hour. Place in a cold oven. Turn oven to 400 degrees and bake 15 minutes. Reduce heat to 350 degrees and bake 20 minutes longer, or until loaves sound hollow when tapped. Remove bread from pans, and cool loaves on a wire rack.

TO STORE: Bread loaves will keep, well-wrapped, for 6–9 months in the freezer.

PACKAGING TIP: Loaves of whole wheat bread are really beautiful on their own, tucked inside a new ceramic loaf pan, or into a grapevine basket lined with a fresh plaid napkin. For Christmas, wrap in clear cellophane paper, then secure cellophane with gauzy gold ribbon.

½ teaspoon
dry mustard

•

1 teaspoon
warm water

•

3 to 3¼ cups
unbleached
all-purpose flour

•

1½ teaspoons salt

•

1 teaspoon coarsely
ground black pepper

•

1 cup low-fat milk

•

3 ounces Cheddar
cheese, shredded
(about ¾ cup)

•

1 tablespoon
active dry yeast
(a 1 ¼-ounce
package)

•

1 tablespoon sugar

•

1 tablespoon
vegetable oil

•

1 egg

•

2 tablespoons
butter, melted

BLACK PEPPER CHEESE BREAD BOULES

In a small mixing bowl, dissolve dry mustard in warm water. In a separate bowl, combine 3 cups of flour with salt and pepper. Warm milk in the microwave oven or on top of the stove. Shred cheese.

In a large mixing bowl or bowl of food processor fitted with a steel blade, combine warmed milk, yeast, sugar, and oil. Stir or process until combined. Add egg and mix well.

Add mustard and flour mixtures. Dough should come together nicely in a mass. (Add up to ¼ cup flour if needed to stiffen dough.) Pour in cheese and incorporate into dough. Turn dough out onto a floured surface and knead, adding more flour as needed. Knead 10 minutes by hand, or for a minute or two in the food processor.

Place dough in a slightly oiled bowl and turn dough to coat all sides. Cover and let rise in a warm place—the back of a gas stove or a warm bathroom—until doubled in bulk, about 1 hour. About 15 minutes before baking, preheat oven to 375 degrees.

Punch dough down and shape into 2 rounds, tucking dough under around bottom edges so that it is nice and neat. Place rounds on opposite ends of a slightly oiled baking sheet. Cover with a light tea towel and let rise in a warm place until doubled, about 1 hour.

Brush risen loaves carefully and lightly with melted butter. Place in oven on middle rack and bake until rounds are golden brown and sound hollow when removed from the pan and tapped on the bottom, about 40 minutes. Cool on a rack before slicing.

TO STORE: Let bread rounds cool completely on rack. Wrap securely in aluminum foil and then slide loaves into a zipper-lock freezer bag. Freeze. These will keep for 6–9 months with little flavor loss.

PACKAGING TIP: Tie loaves in baker's parchment paper or burlap and secure with kitchen twine or off-white raffia. If you want to give more than one boule, stack them on top of each other and tie them together with some wide silk ribbon. Then, tuck into a deep gift bag lined with a new tea towel.

Makes 2 small loaves

•

Preparation time:
2 hours, 30 minutes

Cooking time:
40 minutes

This is one of those recipes that evolved. I found a terrific recipe for yeast bread—and then started experimenting. The variations are really endless—I also sometimes add a tablespoon of minced fresh basil or thyme when they are fresh from the garden. To save time and to make a more visually appealing gift, shape the dough into balls like you might find at a French bakery.

Makes 1 large loaf or
2 medium loaves
•
Preparation time:
20 minutes

Cooking time:
50 to 60 minutes for
large loaves, 40 to 45
minutes for medium
•
♥ Low-fat selection

When my father was recovering from a stroke, Margaret Milam brought him a loaf of this moist bread and a jar full of her special pimento cheese. Margaret says she obtained this recipe from her mother who used to bake it, then spread with softened cream cheese between slices to create what is known in genteel circles as "finger sandwiches."

MARGARET'S DATE NUT BREAD

Preheat oven to 325 degrees. Grease and flour a 9 by 5-inch loaf pan or two smaller pans.

In a 2-quart saucepan placed over medium-high heat, add water and stir in soda. Halve dates lengthwise and stir into water. Stir in butter. Bring mixture to a boil, then remove from heat and stir until butter melts. Let cool in pan for 20 minutes. Mash slightly with a potato masher.

Meanwhile, whisk together flour, sugar, and pinch of salt in a large mixing bowl. Make a well in center. Pour in cooled date mixture, beaten egg, and vanilla. Stir to combine ingredients well. Fold in pecans.

Pour batter into prepared pan. Bake until loaf sets, about 50–60 minutes for large loaf, 40–45 minutes for medium loaves.

Let bread cool in pan for 15 minutes, then turn out onto racks to cool completely before wrapping.

To store: Wrap cooled loaves in foil and then slip foil-wrapped loaves into zipper-lock freezer bags. Freeze. These will store for 6–9 months.

Packaging tip: Tuck a loaf inside a gift basket that might also include a jar of homemade pimento cheese (page 50) and a jar of fresh old-fashioned applesauce (page 49). On its own, a large loaf of date bread is elegant simply wrapped in parchment paper and tied with a wide gold or nut-brown ribbon.

1 cup water
•
1 teaspoon
baking soda
•
1 8-ounce package
(1 cup) pitted dates
•
$^1/_4$ cup butter
•
$1^1/_2$ cups
all-purpose flour
•
1 cup sugar
•
Pinch salt
•
1 egg, beaten
•
2 teaspoons
vanilla extract
•
1 cup chopped pecans

The Italians dip crunchy cookies called biscotti into sweet wine and coffee. Biscotti are often flavored with anise or hazelnuts, but I find people go mad over biscotti when they are simply seasoned with toasted fresh pecans and a little orange rind. If you can't locate pecans, substitute almonds.

**Makes about
16 biscotti**
•
**Preparation time:
25 minutes**
•
**Cooking time:
40 minutes**
•
**Cooling time:
1 to 2 hours**

ORANGE PECAN BISCOTTI

$^3/_4$ cup pecan pieces
•
$1^1/_4$ cups
all-purpose flour
•
$1^1/_2$ teaspoons
baking powder
•
$^1/_4$ teaspoon salt
•
$^1/_4$ cup
unsalted butter,
softened
•
$^1/_4$ cup plus 2
tablespoons sugar
•
$^1/_4$ teaspoon
vanilla extract
•
1 egg
•
1 teaspoon grated
orange zest

Preheat oven to 350 degrees.

Place pecans in a 9-inch pie pan and toast in oven about 5–7 minutes, or until pecans are deep brown and glossy. Watch carefully so pecans don't burn. Chop finely and set aside.

Sift together flour, baking powder, and salt. Set aside.

In large mixing bowl, combine butter and sugar and beat on medium speed until light and fluffy. Beat in vanilla, egg, and orange zest. Fold in dry ingredients and nuts, then mix until thoroughly blended.

Line a baking pan with parchment paper. Form dough into a 3- by 12-inch strip. Mound dough up slightly along center of strip so that sliced biscotti will be slightly thicker in the middle.

Bake on middle rack until light golden, about 18–20 minutes. Remove pan from oven and let cookie loaf cool 10 minutes. Reduce oven temperature to 300 degrees.

Either on the pan or on a cutting board, slice loaf of dough diagonally into $^1/_4$-inch slices. You should have between 12 and 16 strips. Turn strips so that cut side is down. Spread out on pan.

Return pan to oven and bake 20 minutes, turning cookies over halfway through baking. Then, turn off oven and let cookies cool 1–2 hours in oven with heat off.

The cookies should be quite crisp when cooled.

TO STORE: Keep in an airtight container. These can be prepared up to 2 weeks in advance.

PACKAGING TIP: Biscotti are attractive stored upright in a glass container. They also look wonderful on a beautiful plate, so keep your eyes open for one at a flea market. For an extra special gift, package some biscotti along with premium coffee beans, dried orange potpourri, loose mango-scented tea, or good English cocoa.

Makes 6 dozen

•

Preparation time:
45 minutes to 1 hour

•

Chilling time:
2 to 3 hours

•

Cooking time:
25 minutes

Pecan tassies are nothing new—miniature bites of intensely rich pecan pie. But you might never have thought of them as a gift idea. They're ideal for making in a big batch and freezing for gifts in the months ahead. Drizzle melted chocolate—white or dark—across the tops after baking the tassies for a little extra panache.

PECAN TASSIES

FOR THE CRUST: Cut cream cheese and butter into 1-inch cubes and place in food processor or electric mixer, beating to combine well. If you use the food processor, turn mixture out into a large mixing bowl. Add flour a little at a time, incorporating it with a wooden spoon until mixture gets so stiff you cannot work any more flour in. Then use your well-scrubbed fingers to mix.

Form dough into a ball, dust with flour, and wrap well in plastic wrap. Refrigerate 2–3 hours.

Remove dough from refrigerator and form into 1-inch balls. Press balls into $1^1/_2$-inch wide ungreased muffin tins to form small tart shells. Set aside.

Preheat oven to 350 degrees.

FOR THE FILLING: Melt the butter. Combine melted butter with eggs, sugar, salt, vanilla, and pecans. Fill each dough-lined muffin tin with about 1 teaspoon of filling mixture. Bake 25 minutes, or until crust turns golden brown and filling has set. Remove pans from oven and let tassies rest for 20 minutes, then remove to a rack to continue cooling.

TO STORE: Pecan tassies will keep up to a week in the refrigerator in a zipper-lock bag. Or, line them up between layers of parchment paper in a plastic freezer container and freeze for up to 6 months.

PACKAGING TIP: Secure tassies in plastic wrap, then tuck inside a decorative gift bag, or present in a gift miniature muffin tin with a recipe card attached.

57

CRUST:
16 ounces regular
or reduced-fat
cream cheese

•

2 cups butter
or margarine

•

4 cups
all-purpose flour

FILLING:
3 tablespoons butter

•

3 eggs

•

$2^1/_2$ cups dark
brown sugar

•

1 teaspoon salt

•

$^1/_2$ teaspoon
vanilla extract

•

$1^1/_2$ cups coarsely
chopped pecans

CAKE:

2 cups
all-purpose flour

•

2 cups sugar

•

1 cup margarine

•

4 heaping tablespoons
unsweetened cocoa

•

1 cup water

•

$^1/_3$ cup buttermilk

•

2 eggs, beaten

•

1 teaspoon
baking soda

•

1 teaspoon
vanilla extract

ICING:

$^1/_2$ cup butter

•

4 heaping tablespoons
unsweetened cocoa

•

$^1/_3$ cup whole milk

•

One 16-ounce box
confectioners' sugar

•

$^3/_4$ cup chopped
pecans, toasted

Makes 20 servings

•

**Preparation time:
30 minutes**

•

**Cooking time:
25 minutes**

In my family, no get-together seems complete without chocolate sheet cake. As self-proclaimed connoisseurs, we have settled on this recipe as the best. It's based on cocoa and buttermilk, and it's like the popular cola cake but not so sweet. This recipe came home with me years ago, and our family dubbed it Georgia Sheet Cake because I was living in Georgia at the time.

GEORGIA SHEET CAKE

Preheat oven to 350 degrees. Grease and flour a 9 by 13-inch baking pan.

FOR THE CAKE: In a large mixing bowl, stir together flour and sugar. Set aside.

Place margarine, cocoa, and water in a small saucepan over medium-high heat and just bring to a boil, stirring constantly. Remove from heat and stir. Pour hot cocoa mixture over dry ingredients and stir well to combine.

Add buttermilk, beaten eggs, soda, and vanilla to cocoa mixture. Stir well to combine all ingredients.

Pour batter into prepared pan and bake about 25 minutes, or until cake tests done and just begins to pull away from sides of the pan. Place pan on rack and let cool.

FOR THE ICING: You must toast the pecans before sprinkling on top—no ifs, ands, or buts! Turn off oven. Place nuts in a small pie tin and place in oven to toast while cake cools a bit and you prepare the icing. (Watch the nuts carefully—they can burn easily!)

Place butter in a 2-quart saucepan over medium-high heat and stir until melted. Remove pan from heat. Stir in cocoa until completely dissolved. Stir in milk. Pour in confectioners' sugar and stir well to combine so that icing is smooth and satiny.

Spread icing over cooled cake with spatula. Sprinkle toasted pecans on top.

TO STORE: This cake keeps well, but it cuts better after it has been chilled. Wrapped in heavy-duty aluminum foil or sealed in a sturdy plastic container, it will keep in the freezer for 6–9 months.

PACKAGING TIP: This cake is best transported in the pan in which it was baked. If possible, bake it in a gift pan or bake and give in a disposable aluminum foil pan. Cover with plastic wrap or the lid to the pan and attach a copy of the recipe. If you are planning to give only a portion of the cake, chill it before slicing. Arrange squares in a parchment-lined cake tin or sturdy plastic container and secure the lid tightly.

One of the best ways to use fresh autumn apples is in this stunning, substantial cake, baked in a tube pan and coated with a mock-caramel glaze. It really doesn't matter what type of apple you choose, but the firmer, tarter ones tend to have better flavor after cooking. I have even substituted fresh pears, which make a more delicate, softer-textured cake.

CARAMEL-GLAZED APPLE CAKE

Preheat oven to 325 degrees. Lightly grease and flour a 10-inch tube pan.

FOR THE CAKE: Combine sugars and oil in large bowl of electric mixer. Mix well on medium speed for 3–4 minutes. Add eggs, one at a time, beating well after each addition. Sift together flour, cinnamon, soda, nutmeg, and salt. Add dry ingredients to batter and mix well. Fold in apples, walnuts if desired, and vanilla, mixing well.

Pour batter into pan and bake on middle rack of oven until cake tests done and begins to pull away from the sides of the pan, about 1 hour and 15 minutes. Remove from oven and let cake cool in pan 25 minutes before inverting onto cake platter. Meanwhile, prepare glaze.

FOR THE GLAZE: Combine butter or margarine, sugars, cream, and vanilla in a small saucepan and bring to a boil over medium-high heat. Let boil 1 minute. Remove pan from heat.

Poke a few holes in top of cake with a bamboo skewer or fork, and spoon glaze over warm cake. Let it dribble into holes and down sides of the cake. Let cool completely before slicing.

TO STORE: This cake is moist and will keep, well wrapped, in the refrigerator for 3–4 weeks. Wrapped in heavy-duty foil, the cake will keep for up to 6 months in the freezer.

PACKAGING TIP: Place cake into a brown paper grocery sack you have cut down to about a third of its height, and then punch a row of holes about an inch from the top edge. Lace the holes with some narrow grosgrain ribbon, and pull together into a bow. (This is very much like lacing shoes.)

Makes 1 cake, about 16 servings

•

Preparation time: 20 minutes

•

Cooking time: 1 hour, 15 minutes

•

Equipment needed: 10-inch tube pan

GLAZE:

3 tablespoons butter or margarine

•

3 tablespoons light brown sugar

•

3 tablespoons sugar

•

3 tablespoons whipping cream

•

$^1/_2$ teaspoon vanilla extract

CAKE:

$1^1/_2$ cups sugar

•

$^1/_2$ cup light brown sugar

•

$1^1/_2$ cups vegetable oil

•

3 eggs

•

3 cups all-purpose flour

•

2 teaspoons cinnamon

•

1 teaspoon baking soda

•

$^1/_2$ teaspoon ground nutmeg

•

$^1/_2$ teaspoon salt

•

$3^1/_2$ cups chopped raw peeled apples (cut into 1-inch chunks)

•

1 cup chopped English or black walnuts or pecans, optional

•

2 teaspoons vanilla extract

WINTER

Once Thanksgiving platters have been put away,
it is time to start planning—and cooking—for the
upcoming holidays. Be prepared for all the holiday
get-togethers, gift-giving, and family visits by taking
advantage of the very best winter has to offer!

Winter's fresh citrus plays an important part in
this section; recipes range from orange marmalade to
orange currant scones. I've also included some
appetizers to give to any veteran entertainers on your
list. But most of these recipes are sweet—sugar and
gingerbread cookies, toffee and truffles, and cakes
galore, including persimmon, chocolate, and orange.
So forget about making the same old fruitcake!

WINTER'S
DECORATIVE INSPIRATIONS

BOXWOOD BRANCHES
EVERGREENS
HOLLY
IVY
MAGNOLIA LEAVES
PAPERWHITES
RED-TWIG DOGWOOD
WHITE CABBAGE
GRAPEFRUIT
JERUSALEM ARTICHOKES
ORANGES
PERSIMMONS
TANGELOS
TANGERINES
TURNIPS
KUMQUATS

Makes about 6 pints

•

Preparation time:
15 minutes

•

Cooking time:
2 hours

•

Equipment needed:
Microwave oven
Sterilized jars

•

♥ Low-fat selection

JULIE'S ORANGE MARMALADE

2 pounds
thin-skinned oranges
(about 5 medium),
mixed varieties (you
may substitute 2 limes
for one orange if you
are using all sweet-
juice oranges),
well scrubbed

•

1 lemon, well
scrubbed

•

6 cups water

•

7 cups sugar

Wash fruit well. Dry and cook in the microwave oven on high power for 2 minutes, or until fruit has warmed up. (The oranges are more juicy when warm.)

Cut fruit in quarters and remove seeds. (Julie saves the seeds and wraps them up in cheesecloth. She then simmers this bag of seeds along with the marmalade and removes it before turning into jars.)

In four or five batches, place fruit quarters in the bowl of a food processor fitted with a steel blade. Process with short on-off pulses until fruit is chopped to your liking. You may do this by hand if you don't have a food processor. Julie prefers a coarse marmalade; I prefer one that is a little finer, but with some chunks.

Turn fruit and juice into an extra-large, microwave-safe mixing bowl. Stir in water.

Place bowl in microwave oven set at high power and cook 50 minutes, uncovered. Stir fruit several times during this period.

Stir in sugar carefully. Heat, uncovered, on high power for another 50–60 minutes, stirring occasionally, until marmalade produces a scum and then takes on a translucent, glistening appearance. Skim scum layer off the top with a spoon and discard.

Carefully, remove bowl from microwave oven. Remove cheesecloth sack of seeds if they were placed in the mixing bowl. Ladle mixture into hot, sterilized jars. Wipe rims and adjust lids and seal. Let cool on the kitchen counter for several hours, then store in the refrigerator.

TO STORE: Store in refrigerator for 6–9 months. To store on the pantry shelf, follow the directions for water-bath canning, (page 80), for 5 minutes.

PACKAGING TIP: Buy pretty jars for this marmalade. Use the French canning jars or Weck jars (page 80), or the plain Ball jelly jars. Don't wrap in tissue or paper of any kind—the beautiful color of the marmalade will be hidden from view! Tie a pretty yellow or gold ribbon around the rim of the jar. Do as Julie Buchanan did and tuck the marmalade inside a small basket with a jar of the Lemon Curd (page 16), or add a dozen of Flowerree's Overnight Rolls (page 18).

**Makes about 2 dozen
6-inch ribbons or
4 dozen 1-inch
cheese straws**

•

**Preparation time:
25 minutes**

**Cooking time:
8 minutes**

•

**Equipment needed:
Food processor**

You can vary the dough of Kren Teren's ribbons by adding seasonings of your choice. I usually add some curry powder and garlic, and Tabasco sauce adds a zesty touch. If you don't have a cookie press, just roll the dough and cut into rounds, squares, or strips.

KREN'S CHEESE RIBBONS

4 ounces extra-sharp
Cheddar cheese
(about 1 cup)

•

1 cup all-purpose flour

•

$^1/_2$ teaspoon salt

•

$^1/_4$ teaspoon
cayenne pepper, or
more to taste

•

$^1/_4$ teaspoon
curry powder

•

$^1/_8$ teaspoon
garlic powder

•

$^1/_4$ cup
unsalted butter

•

Dash of Tabasco

•

1 egg, beaten

Preheat oven to 425 degrees.

Shred cheese in food processor fitted with shredding blade. Remove shredding blade and insert steel blade. Place flour, salt, and seasonings in processor bowl along with shredded cheese. Process until well combined. Distribute $^1/_4$ cup butter around work bowl and process with short on-off pulses until mixture looks like cornmeal. Add egg and process until mixture comes together in a ball. Remove dough to a work surface.

Leave the dough as it is if you are going to roll it by hand. Roll dough to a little less than $^1/_4$-inch thickness and stamp into rounds or cut into 1-inch squares. Place on ungreased baking sheet.

If you are going to extrude dough through a cookie press, knead in about 1 tablespoon water if needed—dough should be the consistency of cookie dough. Extrude in 1- to 1$^1/_2$-inch wide strips that are about 6 inches long onto an ungreased baking sheet.

Bake 7–8 minutes, or until lightly browned. Remove to a rack to cool, then package.

TO STORE: While you can store baked cheese ribbons in a lidded container in the freezer for up to 6 months, you'll have better success if you freeze the unbaked dough. It will keep for 6–9 months. Let thaw overnight in the refrigerator before rolling and cutting.

PACKAGING TIP: Do as Kren does and wrap these in plastic bags and then tie with raffia ribbons. Other possibilities: place cheese ribbons in a cookie tin lined with waxed paper, or present them in a useful, reusable vessel—like a long plastic spaghetti storage container with lid. The possibilities are endless!

These miniature hot cheese puffs really are dreamy, especially if you've got a sackful of them in your freezer to heat up for an instant hors d'oeuvre. Give them in their frozen state to a friend who entertains frequently. Vary the recipe by using whatever sturdy bread you've got on hand and whatever combination of hard and soft cheeses are in the refrigerator. If you can locate salt-rising bread, it provides marvelous flavor.

**Makes about 50
cheese puffs**
•
**Preparation time:
30 minutes**
•
**Freezing time:
Overnight**
•
**Cooking time:
10 minutes**

CHEESE DREAMS

Trim crusts from the bread. Cut bread into 1-inch cubes and set aside.

In a 2-quart saucepan, melt butter over low heat. Add cheeses and let cook, stirring constantly, over low heat until cheeses just melt. Don't overheat or cheeses will harden and you'll have a mess. Add mustard, cayenne pepper, and salt. Stir and remove from heat.

Beat egg whites until stiff peaks form. Fold whites into cheese mixture.

Spear bread cubes with a fork or skewer and dip into cheese mixture until well coated. Arrange cubes on a baking sheet and freeze, uncovered, until firm. Overnight works best.

To STORE: Transfer frozen bread cubes to a zipper-lock bag where they will keep for up to 6 months in freezer.

To BAKE: Place frozen bread cubes on a baking sheet and bake at 400 degrees for 10 minutes. Serve with a bowl of chutney for dipping.

PACKAGING TIP: Present these bread cubes frozen in their zipper-lock bag. Package them in a basket with a jar of Cranberry Chutney (page 48) or Jezebel Sauce (page 66), and give instructions for heating and serving the cheese puffs with the chutney or sauce.

1 pound unsliced sturdy bread (sourdough, French, rye, wheat, etc.)
•
$^{1}/_{2}$ cup butter or margarine
•
$^{1}/_{4}$ cup shredded mozzarella cheese
•
$^{1}/_{4}$ cup shredded sharp Cheddar cheese
•
$^{1}/_{4}$ cup shredded Swiss cheese
•
3 ounces cream cheese, softened (low-fat works fine)
•
$^{1}/_{2}$ teaspoon dry mustard
•
$^{1}/_{8}$ teaspoon cayenne pepper, or more to taste
•
$^{1}/_{8}$ teaspoon salt
•
2 egg whites

No one knows the exact origin of this sweet and hot sauce. My aunt, Louise Grissim, gave me a jar of this intriguing sauce one Christmas. We found it was the topper for a most irresistible and impromptu hors d'oeuvre—Jezebel Sauce over cream cheese with crunchy wheat crackers. It also makes a terrific glaze for grilled salmon and is just plain good straight from the jar.

**Makes four
8-ounce jars**

•

**Preparation time:
10 minutes**

•

**Equipment needed:
Blender or food
processor**

•

♥ **Low-fat selection**

LOUISE'S JEZEBEL SAUCE

One 18-ounce jar
apricot preserves
(about 2 cups)

•

One 18-ounce jar
apple jelly (about 2
cups)

•

One 5-ounce jar
prepared horseradish
(about $^2/_3$ cup)

•

1 ounce dry mustard
(2 tablespoons)

•

1 teaspoon coarsely
ground black pepper

Combine apricot preserves, apple jelly, horseradish, mustard, and pepper in a blender or food processor fitted with steel blade. Pulse until ingredients are combined and smooth. Pour into sterilized jars and seal. Serve over cream cheese with crackers or as a glaze for fish or pork.

To store: This sauce keeps unopened in the refrigerator for up to 6 months. If opened, it will keep in the refrigerator for 6 weeks.

Packaging tip: Package this sauce in 8-ounce jelly jars. On the label include instructions on refrigerating and serving with cream cheese and crackers. Wrap red or green cellophane or tissue paper up around jar and secure around rim with gold ribbon.

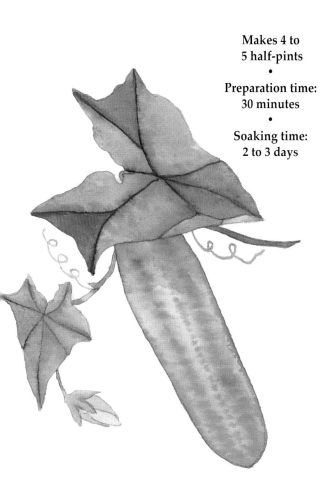

Makes 4 to
5 half-pints
•
Preparation time:
30 minutes
•
Soaking time:
2 to 3 days

Equipment needed:
Nonaluminum, extra-
large mixing bowl
•
♥ Low-fat selection

When you taste these crisp, sweet pickles, you'll never believe they came from a three-ingredient recipe that pulls together in the refrigerator while you're away. And don't worry about cheating because you're using premade pickles—the taste of these pickles will definitely soothe your conscience!

EASY BREAD AND BUTTER PICKLES

Slice pickles $1/4$-inch thick and layer pickles alternately with sugar in a nonaluminum, extra-large mixing bowl.

Cover with plastic wrap. Place in refrigerator and let pickles marinate for 2–3 days. Stir several times each day, so that sugar dissolves in liquid.

At the end of soaking time, pack into clean half-pint jars, seal, and refrigerate.

TO STORE: Pickles will keep in the refrigerator for 4 to 5 months.

PACKAGING TIP: Choose the lovely French canning jars with plastic tops available at The Home Place or Williams-Sonoma stores. Or, pack the pickles in the attractive Weck tulip jars (pint) or mold jars. See page 80 for information on jars.

One 32-ounce jar
whole dill pickles,
drained
•
Two 16-ounce jars
whole sour pickles,
drained
•
4 cups sugar

Ingredients

$^1/_2$ cup currants

•

$^1/_2$ cup orange juice (fresh squeezed, if available)

•

1 tablespoon Grand Marnier

•

$^1/_4$ cup buttermilk

•

1 egg

•

1 teaspoon vanilla extract

•

1 tablespoon orange zest

•

$^1/_2$ cup sugar

•

$3^1/_2$ cups all-purpose flour

•

4 teaspoons baking powder

•

$^1/_2$ teaspoon baking soda

•

$^1/_4$ teaspoon salt

•

$^1/_2$ cup unsalted butter, cut into 16 pieces

Makes 40 scones

•

Preparation time: 30 minutes

•

Cooking time: 8 minutes

•

Equipment needed: Food processor or pastry blender

Nestled in the foothills of the Smoky Mountains in East Tennessee is an elegant inn known as Blackberry Farm. Here the chef, John Fleer, turns heads with what he calls "foothills cuisine." Fleer dabbles in the foods of a variety of foothills, such as the Basque region of Spain, always striving to find that middle ground between comforting and elegant. These scones are a good example of that perfect middle ground.

ORANGE CURRANT SCONES

Place currants in a small mixing bowl. Warm orange juice over low heat for a few minutes, and then pour over currants. Add Grand Marnier. Let soak 15 minutes.

Drain currants, reserving currants and orange juice mixture in separate bowls. Whisk buttermilk, egg, and vanilla extract into orange juice mixture. Set aside.

In bowl of food processor fitted with a steel blade or in a mixing bowl, combine orange zest and sugar. Pulse a few times in processor, or combine by hand with a pastry blender in mixing bowl. Add flour, baking powder, soda, and salt to sugar mixture. Pulse a few times or stir to combine. Distribute butter pieces over dry ingredients and either pulse or combine with a pastry blender until butter looks like crumbs.

Preheat oven to 400 degrees. Stir wet ingredients into dry ingredients. Fold in currants. Divide mixture into 10 balls, roughly 3 ounces each. With lightly floured hands, pat balls into 1-inch thick rounds, then cut each ball into 4 quarters. Place quarters on lightly greased baking sheets and bake about 8 minutes, or until scones are lightly browned. Brush with melted butter when they come out of the oven and serve warm with hot tea.

To store: Cooled, baked scones can be frozen for up to 9 months. Wrap first in foil, then place the foil package in a zipper-lock bag. Reheat or thaw to room temperature in the foil.

Packaging tip: These scones make a nice companion to a tin of good-quality loose tea or a bag of premium roasted coffee beans in a napkin-lined basket. Or select a beautiful china teapot and fill it with the scones.

CRISP GINGERBREAD STARS

FOR COOKIES: Combine butter and sugar in the large bowl of an electric mixer. Beat on medium-high speed until well combined. Add egg and beat until light and fluffy. Fold in orange zest and corn syrup and mix well. Remove beaters.

Sift flour, soda, cinnamon, ginger, cloves, and salt together in a second bowl, then fold them into creamed mixture with a spatula. Chill dough at least 2–3 hours.

Preheat oven to 375 degrees. Lightly flour a work surface and roll out dough to $^1/_4$-inch thickness. Cut into stars and place at least 1 inch apart on ungreased baking sheets. Work quickly with the dough because it is buttery and will get sticky.

Bake on the middle rack for 8–10 minutes, or until browned. Cool for 1 minute on pan, then remove cookies to a wire rack to cool.

FOR ICING: Combine confectioners' sugar and water in a small bowl until smooth. Use a knife to spread cooled cookies with icing, or use a pastry bag with tip to pipe icing around edges of stars. Let icing dry before storing.

TO STORE: Cookies will keep in a tightly covered tin at room temperature for about 2 weeks. For longer storage, freeze them in a tightly covered container for up to 6 months.

PACKAGING TIP: When these cookies are iced, they can get a little messy, so don't try to stack them on top of each other in a cookie tin. Instead, spread out on a disposable silver paper tray and lightly cover with plastic wrap. If desired, decorate the tray with silver ribbon and stars.

**Makes about
5 dozen stars**

•

**Preparation time:
45 minutes**

•

**Cooking time:
8 to 10 minutes**

COOKIES:
1 cup unsalted
butter, softened

•

$1^1/_2$ cups sugar

•

1 egg

•

4 teaspoons grated
orange zest

•

2 tablespoons
dark corn syrup

•

$3^1/_4$ cups
all-purpose flour

•

2 teaspoons baking
soda

•

2 teaspoons cinnamon

•

1 teaspoon
ground ginger

•

$^1/_2$ teaspoon
ground cloves

•

$^1/_2$ teaspoon salt

ICING:
2 cups
confectioners' sugar

•

2 tablespoons water,
or as needed

This is the best gingerbread cookie recipe I have tested. It's not cardboard thick and tough, but crisp and buttery and delicately seasoned with orange zest, cinnamon, ginger, and cloves. I like to cut the dough into stars, but you could just as easily press out gingerbread people. If you do, cut out a hole at the top of their heads with a drinking straw before baking. Once baked and decorated, you can run a ribbon through the hole and hang the cookie as an ornament.

Christmas just doesn't seem like Christmas without carefully decorated sugar cookies on a silver tray. (And for Valentine's Day, these cookies are stunning cut into hearts and sprinkled with red and pink sugars.) Kathleen, my older daughter, loves to help decorate with sprinkles. To save time when little ones are helping you, make the dough the day or night before, wrap in plastic wrap, and chill. Then you're ready to cut, decorate, and bake.

Makes about 5 dozen

•

Preparation time:
15 minutes

•

Chilling time:
1 hour or overnight

•

Cooking time:
10 to 12 minutes

COOKIES:
1 cup
unsalted butter,
softened

•

1 cup sugar

•

2 eggs

•

2 teaspoons
vanilla extract

•

3 cups
all-purpose flour

•

Strawberry or
raspberry jam (for
Thumbprint version)

•

Chopped pecans,
if desired (for
Thumbprint version)

EDIBLE PAINT:
2 egg yolks

•

Assorted colors of
food coloring

•

$1/_2$ teaspoon water

CONFECTIONERS'
SUGAR ICING:

•

1 cup sifted
confectioners' sugar

•

1 to 2 tablespoons
low-fat milk, warmed

•

Assorted colors
of food coloring,
if desired

•

Almond extract,
if desired

KATHLEEN'S SUGAR COOKIES

FOR COOKIES: Beat butter and sugar together in a mixing bowl until light and fluffy. Add eggs and vanilla. Beat well. Stir in flour. Cover and chill at least 1 hour, preferably overnight.

Preheat oven to 350 degrees. Working with a little of the dough at a time, roll it out on a floured surface to about $1/_8$-inch thickness. Keep remaining dough chilled. Cut with desired cookie cutters and transfer carefully to an ungreased baking sheet, spacing an inch apart. If there is enough room in your refrigerator, chill baking sheets for 5 minutes before baking. This helps cookies retain their shape if you've overworked the dough or the kitchen is hot.

Place cookies in oven and bake 10–12 minutes, or until golden brown. Cool on racks.

TO DECORATE: If you want to add an edible paint, do so before baking. If you are using colored sugars, brush cookies with a little egg white before sprinkling on decoration. If you are going to frost with a powdered sugar icing, bake cookies first.

For EDIBLE PAINT (alias Paintbrush Cookies): Mix 2 egg yolks and $1/_2$ teaspoon water in a small bowl. Divide mixture among several small cups. Tint each cup with a different food coloring. Paint cookies with small, clean, new paint brushes. If paint thickens up, add a little water. Then bake as directed.

For CONFECTIONERS' SUGAR ICING: Combine 1 cup sifted confectioners' sugar and 1 to 2 tablespoons or more warm low-fat milk, until desired consistency. Tint, if desired, with food coloring. You can also add a dash of almond flavoring, if desired. If frosting gets too runny, add more confectioners' sugar. Frost baked cookies.

For THUMBPRINT COOKIES: Prepare dough as recipe directs. Preheat oven to 375 degrees. After chilling dough, shape into 1-inch balls. If desired, roll balls in finely chopped pecans before pressing and baking. Arrange balls about 2 inches apart on ungreased baking sheet. Using your thumb, make a depression in the center of each ball. Bake 10 minutes. Remove from oven, fill each cookie with a little strawberry or raspberry jam. Return cookies

to oven for about 4 minutes, or until lightly browned. Makes about 5 dozen.

For a tasty variation, fill the thumbprints with Lemon Curd (page 16) after they have cooled. (Refrigerate for longer storage.)

To STORE: Keep in a tightly covered tin at room temperature for up to 2 weeks, or store in a tightly covered container in the freezer for up to 6 months. For best results, freeze the unbaked dough, then let thaw in the refrigerator before rolling and cutting.

PACKAGING TIP: These beautiful cookies need little adornment from packaging. I have simply wrapped up a dozen in plastic wrap, then overwrapped them with green cellophane and secured a gold organdy ribbon around the top. Or, stash them in a festive cookie tin that has been lined with parchment paper, or pile them into a pretty basket or onto a sturdy paper plate.

Because of the subtle, sophisticated statement that chocolate truffles make, and because you have to pay dearly for them in chocolate shops, you'd expect them to be trouble to make at home, right? Wrong. Truffles are one of the easier candies to construct because you don't need a fancy thermometer—if you have patience, some good chocolate, and a lucky recipient to praise you for these sinful treats, you can make wonderful truffles!

Makes about 20

•

Preparation time:
1 $^{1}/_{2}$ hours

•

Chilling time:
About 4 hours

VALENTINE'S TRUFFLES

2 oranges, preferably organic, or very well scrubbed

•

$^{3}/_{4}$ cup whipping cream

•

8 ounces semisweet or bittersweet chocolate, finely chopped

•

$^{2}/_{3}$ cup ground lightly toasted pecans, unsweetened ground cocoa, or flaked coconut

Pare the orange-colored part of the orange peel in long strips using a sharp vegetable peeler. Place strips in a 1$^{1}/_{2}$-quart saucepan along with whipping cream. Place pan over medium-high heat and warm until cream just begins to bubble. Remove from heat, cover, and let orange peels rest in cream for 20 minutes. Then, strain cream into a small bowl, pressing orange strips to extract more flavor as cream flows through strainer.

Place chocolate pieces in a medium heatproof bowl. Place strained cream into saucepan over medium-high heat. When it comes to a boil, pour over chocolate. Stir with a whisk until chocolate melts and mixture is smooth. Cool to room temperature.

Cover chocolate mixture with plastic wrap and place in refrigerator until thick enough to spoon out into little mounds. Stir from the sides of the bowl to the center as chocolate will harden first at the sides of the bowl. This thickening process will take from 1 to 2 hours.

Meanwhile, line a baking sheet with aluminum foil.

When chocolate mixture has thickened throughout, spoon mixture into $^{3}/_{4}$-inch mounds and place on foil. Cover with plastic wrap and chill about 20 minutes, or until firm enough to handle.

Roll each mound into a small ball. Pour ground nuts in a shallow bowl. Roll truffles in the nuts when they are still somewhat soft on the outside so that the nuts adhere all over. Place truffles on foil-lined sheet, cover, and chill. If you don't wish to use nuts, you can roll the truffles in unsweetened ground cocoa or flaked coconut.

Truffles need about 2 hours to firm up in the refrigerator after rolling in nuts.

TO STORE: Place in an airtight container in the refrigerator for up to 5 days, or in the freezer for 2–3 months.

PACKAGING TIP: Place each truffle into an individual candy liner or miniature muffin paper liner. Arrange these in something beautiful for your Valentine—a crystal vase, an antique silver box, even a simple cardboard box you have covered with rich, red silk. Tie the container with a silky red ribbon and your truffles are ready to be given.

BEBE'S CHOCOLATE TOFFEE

Liberally butter the shiny side of two 18-inch sheets of aluminum foil.

Place sugar, water, butter, and margarine in a 3-quart saucepan over medium-high heat. Stir mixture occasionally with a wooden spoon, without scraping the sides of the pan, until butter and margarine melt and mixture darkens and thickens and registers 280 degrees on a candy thermometer. This will take from 30–40 minutes.

Add coarsely chopped pecans and begin to stir mixture constantly for about 5 minutes, or until mixture registers 310 degrees on candy thermometer. Be careful not to scrape the sides of the pan.

Pour toffee at once onto one of the buttered sheets of aluminum foil. Spread it out with a metal spatula until it is evenly $^1/_4$-inch thick. Unwrap 6 of the chocolate bars, break into pieces, and carefully scatter on top of hot toffee. As chocolate melts, spread it evenly across toffee with a knife, spreading so it reaches all the edges. Sprinkle with half of the ground pecans.

Cover toffee with buttered side of second sheet of aluminum foil. Tuck in ends and sides so that pecans don't scatter when you flip it over.

Carefully flip toffee over and remove top sheet of aluminum foil. Repeat method described above of placing 6 chocolate bars on top to melt, spread them to edges, and then scatter with remaining ground pecans.

Let toffee cool, uncovered, for 4–5 hours, or until it is hard and chocolate has set. If you are in a hurry you can place the toffee in the refrigerator where it will set in an hour, but be warned—the chocolate doesn't stick to the candy as well this way. Once cooled, break toffee into 1- or 2-inch pieces.

TO STORE: Toffee will keep in metal tins or a zipper-lock bag in a cool place for up to 3 or 4 weeks.

PACKAGING TIP: Enclose toffee pieces in glassine paper envelopes used for stamp collecting, and then arrange the envelopes in a decorative tin or velvet-covered box. Or line a tin or plastic container with waxed or parchment paper and fill with toffee. Secure top of container tightly to keep toffee fresh. My mother likes to wrap portions of toffee in small plastic bags and then tuck these portions into decorative paper sacks. And a last, elegant way to present toffee—place the pieces in clear plastic bags like those used at candy shops or found in the Williams-Sonoma catalog. Secure with a deep moss green velvet ribbon.

Makes 2 $^1/_2$ to 3 pounds

•

**Preparation time:
20 minutes**

•

**Cooking time:
40 to 45 minutes**

•

**Cooling time:
4 to 5 hours**

•

**Equipment needed:
Candy thermometer**

2 cups sugar

•

1 cup water

•

1 cup butter

•

$^1/_2$ cup margarine

•

12 (1.55-ounce each) milk chocolate bars (I usually use Hershey's)

•

1 pound pecans, half coarsely chopped and half ground

This is a spectacular recipe, one my mother has been preparing for Christmas gifts for years. The secret is to take your time. Be careful not to scrape the sides of the pan as the toffee cooks or the toffee won't be smooth and satiny in texture. And try to make toffee on a dry, not rainy, day; for some reason, humidity can spoil homemade candy.

This spectacular chocolate layer cake is appropriately named. It isn't, however, a cake for the faint-hearted or the fat-gram counter. This is for the special someone whose birthday or anniversary falls during winter, or to take along to a holiday caroling party or tree-decking buffet.

Makes a three-tier, 9-inch layer cake
•
Preparation time: 50 minutes to 1 hour

Cooking time: 25 to 30 minutes
•
Equipment needed: Three 9-inch cake pans

PERFECT CHOCOLATE CAKE

CAKE:
1 cup cocoa
•
2 cups boiling water
•
1 cup butter or margarine, softened
•
$2^1/_2$ cups sugar
•
4 eggs
•
$1^1/_2$ teaspoons vanilla extract
•
$2^3/_4$ cups all-purpose flour
•
2 teaspoons baking soda
•
$^1/_2$ teaspoon baking powder
•
$^1/_2$ teaspoon salt

FILLING:
1 cup whipping cream
•
$^1/_4$ cup confectioners' sugar
•
1 teaspoon vanilla extract

FROSTING:
One 6-ounce package semisweet chocolate chips (about $^3/_4$ cup)
•
$^1/_2$ cup half-and-half
•
1 cup butter or margarine
•
$2^1/_2$ cups confectioners' sugar

Preheat oven to 350 degrees. Lightly grease and flour three 9-inch cake pans.

Combine cocoa and boiling water in a small mixing bowl, and stir until smooth. Set aside to cool.

In large bowl of electric mixer, combine butter, sugar, eggs, and vanilla. Beat at medium-high speed for 5 minutes, or until light and fluffy. Combine flour, soda, baking powder, and salt. Add to butter and sugar mixture alternately with cocoa mixture, beating on low speed just until dry ingredients are incorporated. Don't overbeat.

Pour batter into prepared pans. Bake 25–30 minutes or until just done. Don't overbake. Cool in pans 10 minutes, then turn out onto racks to cool completely.

When cool, sandwich cake layers with filling. Then, spread frosting over top and sides of cake. Serve at once, or chill until needed.

For the filling: Combine whipping cream, confectioners' sugar, and vanilla in a mixing bowl. Whip with electric mixer until thick. Chill until needed. Makes about 2 cups.

For the frosting: Place a large bowl of ice in the kitchen sink, making sure the bowl is large enough to support your saucepan. Combine chocolate chips, half-and-half, and butter in a saucepan set over medium heat. Stir until chocolate melts. Remove from heat and stir in confectioners' sugar. Place saucepan in the bowl of ice. Beat with a hand electric mixer or with a wooden spoon until frosting holds its shape and is satiny. Makes about 3 cups.

To store: Because of the cream and butter in this cake recipe, it must be kept refrigerated until served. Leftovers should also be stored in the refrigerator for up to 1 week. The cake may also be frozen for up to 6 months.

Packaging tip: Tuck the cake into a nice white cake box from a local bakery and tie a wide chocolate brown satin ribbon around the box. Include a label with storing instructions and a recipe card, if desired. To make it look Christmas festive, add a sprig of holly or boxwood. If you're giving the cake as a birthday or anniversary gift, don't forget to include candles!

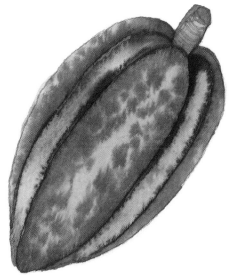

This easy fresh orange cake is just the gift for winter months when all sorts of beautiful oranges are in season. When I was a child, we always had a fresh orange cake on the sideboard at Christmas. This is also expecially nice made with tangerines. Bake in a 9- to 10-inch deep layer cake pan or spoon batter into madeleine molds. Glaze or dust with powdered sugar after baking.

Makes 8 to 10 servings

•

Preparation time: 25 minutes

•

Cooking time: 30 to 35 minutes

•

Equipment needed: Deep 9- or 10-inch layer cake pan or 2 dozen madeleine molds

---

$^1/_2$ cup unsalted butter, softened

•

$^3/_4$ cup granulated sugar

•

2 eggs, separated

•

Grated zest of 2 oranges

•

1$^1/_2$ cups all-purpose flour, sifted after measuring

•

1$^1/_2$ teaspoons baking powder

•

$^1/_4$ teaspoon baking soda

•

$^1/_4$ teaspoon salt

•

$^1/_2$ cup fresh-squeezed orange juice

ORANGE GLAZE:

$^1/_4$ cup fresh-squeezed orange juice

•

$^1/_4$ cup sugar

OR:

Confectioners' sugar (enough to dust cake)

CHRISTMAS ORANGE CAKE

FOR THE CAKE: Preheat oven to 350 degrees. Grease and flour a deep 9- to 10-inch layer pan. Cream butter and gradually add sugar, beating until light. Beat in egg yolks, one at a time. Add orange zest.

In another bowl, combine sifted flour with baking powder, baking soda, and salt, then add these dry ingredients to batter alternately with orange juice. Beat egg whites until stiff and fold them into the batter.

Pour batter into prepared pan. Bake 30–35 minutes, or until sides of cake shrink away from the edges of pan and cake tests done.

Cool 12 minutes in pan, unmold onto a plate, and drizzle with Orange Glaze while cake is still a little warm.

FOR THE ORANGE GLAZE: Combine fresh orange juice and sugar in a small saucepan and simmer for 5 minutes, stirring, until mixture thickens slightly.

ALTERNATIVE "FROSTING": Dust cake(s) with confectioners' sugar.

TO STORE: Freeze in a zipper-lock bag for up to 6 months, or store in the refrigerator for up to a week.

PACKAGING TIP: Tuck this easy orange cake into a basket lined with parchment or white tissue paper. Loosely cover with plastic wrap and secure a deep orange satin ribbon or some orange-dyed raffia around the basket.

Persimmons keep these little cakes moist, and I find they are perfect for slicing at brunch or serving with a glass of eggnog after dinner during the holidays. This cake's combination of bourbon and persimmons may remind you of the intoxicating fruit cakes of Southern heritage. Persimmons are most accessible in the fall and winter months at the supermarket. Buy the large Hachiya or Japanese persimmons or the smaller Fuyu persimmons.

**Makes four
1-pound cakes**
•
**Preparation time:
25 minutes**
•
**Cooking time:
1 hour**

**Equipment needed:
Four 1-pound coffee
tins, 3-cup charlotte
molds, or small
Pyrex bowls**

3 $^1/_2$ cups sifted
all-purpose flour (sifted
before measuring)
•
1 $^1/_2$ teaspoons salt
•
2 teaspoons
baking soda
•
$^1/_2$ teaspoon allspice
•
$^1/_2$ teaspoon
ground nutmeg
•
2 $^1/_4$ cups sugar
•
1 cup unsalted butter
•
4 eggs, lightly beaten
•
$^2/_3$ cup bourbon
•
2 cups persimmon
puree (washed,
unpeeled, mashed ripe
persimmons—about 4)
•
2 cups chopped pecans,
walnuts, or almonds
•
1 $^1/_2$ cups
golden raisins
•
Butter and flour to
prepare tins, molds, etc.

PERSIMMON CAKES

Preheat oven to 350 degrees. Generously butter and flour four 1-pound coffee tins, 3-cup charlotte molds, or small Pyrex bowls. Set aside.

Place flour, salt, soda, allspice, nutmeg, and sugar in a large mixing bowl. Make a well in the center. Melt butter and pour into well along with beaten eggs, bourbon, and persimmon puree. Combine dry and wet ingredients well, then fold in nuts and raisins.

Pour batter into prepared pans until about three-quarters of the way full. Bake 1 hour, or until cakes test done by springing back when you touch them and slightly coming away from the sides of the pan.

Remove pans to a rack to cool 10 minutes, then turn cakes out onto a rack to finish cooling.

To store: Wrap well in foil to store. Persimmon cakes will keep nicely on the kitchen counter for a few days. For longer storage, keep in the refrigerator for 1–2 weeks or in the freezer for up to 6 months.

PACKAGING TIP: Wrap the cakes in aluminum foil or plastic wrap, and then overwrap with bright red cellophane. Pull the edges of the wrap up together then secure the wrap close to the cake with some bright orange satin ribbon (if you're daring) or some tamer green satin ribbon (if you're not so brave!). These cakes also keep well in a decorative tin.

INDEX

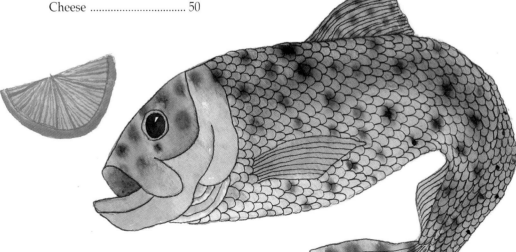

WATER-BATH CANNING METHOD

You can easily extend the shelf life of jams, preserves, and pickles by using the water-bath canning method.

A water bath canner is a large covered cooking pot that ideally has a rack fitted inside. You can use almost any large pot as long as it is deep enough for the water to cover the jars by 1 to 2 inches and still have another 1 to 2 inches of space for the water to boil. The canner should be no more than 4 inches wider than the diameter of the stove's burner so adequate heat reaches all the jars. It also must have a tight-fitting lid and a rack to keep jars from touching the bottom of the pan.

1) Fill the canner with water and bring to a boil over medium-high heat. You'll need 1 to 2 inches of water above the tops of jars; while there is no way to measure precisely, you'll get better with it over time. Have an extra pan of water heating to the side just in case you need to add more.

2) Check the jars. Make sure they have no cracks and that they have been cleaned and then sterilized in boiling water.

3) Pack hot preserves or pickles into jars that are still hot from cleaning. The amount of headspace, or room at the top of the jar, will vary. Check the individual recipe.

4) Wipe the rims of the filled jars with a clean, damp cloth. Seal using two-piece lids. Place the flat part of the lid onto the jar, then screw the band down tightly.

5) Carefully place filled, closed jars on the rack in the canner. Add more boiling water as needed so that the water is 1 to 2 inches over the tops of the jars. If you add more water, pour it between the jars, not directly on them, so the jars don't break.

6) Cover the canner. When the water comes back to a boil, begin counting the processing time. Boil gently for the recommended time in the recipe, adding more boiling water as needed.

7) Use a jar lifter and remove hot jars from the canner onto a rack or a dry tea towel. Let them cool at least 12 hours before storing.

SOURCES

Packaging containers and materials can be found at discount stores, hardware stores, kitchen stores, the local florist and bakery, even the supermarket. But should you want to mail order beautiful jars, here are three sources:

Williams-Sonoma. Call 1-800-541-2233 to order a catalog with a stunning selection of jars, bottles, bins, and papers for year-round packaging.

Glashaus/Weck Home Canning. Call 708-640-6918. This Arlington Heights, IL, firm specializes in beautiful German jars for jellies and pickles and has a variety of canning supplies.

The Container Store. Call 1-800-733-3532 to order THE ULTIMATE GUIDE TO KITCHEN AND PANTRY ORGANIZATION, a catalog offering Spanish glass bottles, plastic tubs, stacking jars, French canning jars, square glass canisters, and more.